D0560642

HOW TO GET ANYONE
TO DO ANYTHING

HOW TO GET ANYONE TO DO ANYTHING

R. PHILIP HANES

with Penelope Niven

TEN SPEED PRESS
Berkeley / Toronto

1⊜

Ten Speed Press
PO Box 7123
Berkeley CA 94707
www.tenspeed.com

Ten Speed books are distributed in Australia by Simon and Schuster
Australia, in Canada by Ten Speed Press Canada, in New Zealand by
Southern Publishers Group, in South Africa by Real Books, in Southeast Asia by Berkeley Books, and in the United Kingdom and Europe
by Airlift Book Company.

Cover and text design by Brad Greene / Greene Design
Frontispiece photo by Lenny Cohen

The Library of Congress cataloging-in-publication data
on file with the publisher.

ISBN 10: 1-58008-667-5
ISBN 13: 987-1-58008-667-7

Printed in the United States of America

First printing, 2006

1 2 3 4 5 – 09 08 07 06

You can accomplish anything
you can dream,
if you can get someone else
to do it.

CONTENTS

FOREWORD

He who would follow all the rest will always end up
second best.
—PIET HEIN

A citizen, a lover of the arts, a champion of the environment, and a businessman, I have in the winter of 2005 celebrated seventy-nine years of building my product line. What I have to offer in this book are the tools for getting things done.

If you stay awake, you will keep learning all of your life. There is a difference between learning and being educated. I spent twenty-five years getting educated; since then I have been learning. Now formal education, mind you, is a good thing—but let's keep it in perspective. My formal education taught me where to find things, how to get useful information, and how to gather enough material to know how to ask questions. My earliest education was centered on the fundamentals: how to survive childhood; how to transmute sissyhood into machismo.

My years from infancy to puberty were full of the normal confusion accompanying an uninformed start-up in a complex environment. I don't think I was spoiled, although I lived in a big house with a Scots nanny and loving parents. I remember significant punishments that included my father beating me with a polo whip. These incidents don't seem so important today, but to a child with an overabundance of energy, a week of house arrest when all my friends were outdoors playing games and going to movies seemed almost unbearable.

I was born with ADHD (attention-deficit hyperactivity disorder), a condition that made me very impatient and often frustrated. I would beat my head on the floor when I couldn't get things to work the way I wanted them. And when I wanted to say something, often my mind raced ahead so fast that I couldn't get my points across. This frustration alone was enough to set me off.

The years from twelve to seventeen, in school and at summer camp, were terrible. I was constantly baited by one particular classmate whom that I deeply disliked. One morning he embarrassed me before my entire class, and I struck him. He instantly assumed the classic boxer's pose. I had never had boxing lessons and, knowing I was totally outclassed, I ran. Everyone laughed. It was my greatest humiliation. At that moment, I decided I had to get with the game.

I studied the most popular guys in school and copied whatever they did that seemed to please others. I learned to play a boogie-woogie on the piano as well as some simple chords to accompany

SNAKES

At Episcopal High School Camp I found myself pursued relentlessly, and the target for various kinds of torments. However, I learned that most of my fellow campers were afraid of snakes. So I studied them assiduously and usually stowed a ring neck or garter snake in my pocket to use as my Excalibur. This early interest developed over several years and by the time I was seventeen I had learned how to catch a snake by grasping it just behind the head. This technique worked even for venomous copperheads and rattlesnakes.

My most exciting catch took place on a boat as my friend Christine Gray's arm was about to touch a ledge on which I spied a sleeping copperhead. I reached over from the rear seat and grabbed it, just behind its head. I held him thus for a good twenty minutes until a glass milk bottle could be found to stuff him into headfirst. Today I am lucky to be married to a woman who has no qualms about draping a ten-foot python over her shoulders.

singers. I took up the ukulele and harmonica. I memorized some jokes. I began studying people to find out how to make friends. I found out that each person required a different approach and so began the start-up for this book. My fifth year at prep school was actually fun and my college years even more so. What I really learned from college was how to find information and people. It was during this time that I subconsciously became a networker. I enjoy connecting people and being connected to them. Usually I bring people together on purpose. But sometimes connections happen out of the blue.

I joined the Navy's ninety-day officer-training course, the V-12 program, at the University of North Carolina in Chapel Hill. But after sixty days, I was transferred to the Naval Reserve Officer Training Corps. I wanted to drop out and just be an able-bodied seaman because all my friends were involved in World War II. Told that this was possible only if I flunked out, I proceeded to do just that, accumulating 3 Fs and 8 Ds. But then the war ended.

Fortunately, my uncle, John Hanes, was on the board of trustees of Yale University and managed to get me enrolled there. My grades were a gentleman's Cs. I joined the glee club and the Whiffenpoofs and sang across America and Europe. My greatest triumph was in Bermuda. My fiancé's stepfather, John Shannon, was vice president in charge of Pan American Airway's passenger travel. In an effort to attract college kids to Bermuda, Pan Am arranged to give free trips

to several Ivy League soccer teams during spring break. I suggested
that he send the Whiffs also. We were given two cottages, three
Jeeps, a bike apiece, and expenses. Our only obligation was to give
two two-hour concerts. The island was ours! No party of any sort
took place without an invitation to us. Perhaps not surprisingly, my
only real memory of that vacation was the night we hosted a joint
barbecue songfest on the beach with the Bermuda-based African-
American singing group, the Talbot Brothers.

Several events still return to mind from my European tour with
the Yale glee club. The Duke and Duchess of Norfolk's debutante
ball was the first really big dance after the war, and to say that it was
a lavish event is an understatement. The Whiffs were the headline
entertainment and notices of our presence were overblown enough
to make us instant celebrities. And it wasn't just our autographs that
the English debs were seeking.

A performance in the Netherlands at a royal palace and with
Queen Wilhelmina in attendance marked my first visit to a royal
residence and my first meeting with a reigning monarch.

A wealthy Yale alumnus living in Helsinki threw a pool party for
us, where the glee club director, Marshall Bartholomew, explained
beforehand that the Finnish custom was to swim naked. On a previous trip, the local girls had observed this custom and were embarrassed when visiting swim-suited Yalis appeared. So this time, we all
lined up buck-naked in the dressing room and made a mad dash into

the pool only to find that our host had given the opposite instructions to the women. Everyone damn near froze waiting for the girls to leave the pool.

I contracted a severe form of flu while touring in Germany and was sent to Goering's Luftwaffe hospital in Frankfurt to recuperate. I asked a nurse, "Whose occupation do you like the best, American or Russian?"

She said she preferred the Russians. "We were told by the Nazis which vocation to choose. I was told to be a nurse. The Russians reinforced that. You Americans say, 'You're free to do whatever you wish,' and I am torn apart wondering if this is what I really want to do."

All this gave me a little bit of Weltanschauung, or understanding of our world. Early childhood unhappiness and disappointments taught me what an underdog faces, while my college years gave me a feeling for the joys of achievement. I guess it was at this point I became an overachiever, no doubt fueled up by the ADHD and an understanding that much could be accomplished by working in harmony with others.

I was married at the age of twenty-four to Joan Humpstone and was in the Navy at twenty-five learning discipline—or at least learning what discipline is. The Korean War put me on a destroyer for eight months, and then I was sent to a naval command code room in Grosvenor Square, London, for two years. This time in London, where Joan and I knew no one, helped build a sound and wonderful foundation for our marriage. After all, there's no better glue for any relationship than the sharing made necessary when two people are in a strange environment and dependent upon each other.

While searching for a house in London, Joan and I stayed for two months at the Ford Hotel in Baker Street just across the way from the mythical residence of Sherlock Holmes. We found a small, furnished carriage house on Montpelier Walk in Knightsbridge about three blocks from the fabled Harrods department store. Our basement had a tiny kitchen and dining room, on the first floor was a living room, the second floor had a master bedroom and the only bathroom, and there were two tiny bedrooms on the third. There was no central heating, so we bought a bale-handled Aladdin kerosene stove and carried it from room to room throughout the winter.

We moved in on a weekend. On Monday morning there was a sharp knocking at the door. A red-faced gentleman asked, "I say, is that your car? Well, you're in my parking spot, which I have had for many years." I asked if he could show me a good parking spot, which he did; and then we invited him in for tea, which he accepted. He turned out to be Lord Colwyn, an Irish peer, who later honored us with a tour and luncheon in the House of Lords.

Joan and I made friends wherever we found them. Back in the states, we belonged to the New York Society of Classical Guitar, an international organization built adoringly around Maestro Andres

Segovia. In London we joined the Philharmonic Society of Classical Guitar. Our best friends were Phil Wrestler, a struggling tailor, and his girlfriend, Wendy. When a black-tie dinner was given for Maestro Segovia, we took them as our guests. Phil made an evening dress for Wendy and borrowed my tux while I wore my naval uniform. At our table was a couple speaking French. Remarking that whenever I hear French spoken I always think of good food, I asked, "What's the best restaurant in London?"

"Ah," said the man, "it is ze Knightsbridge Grill."

Asked why he recommended it, he answered, "Because I am ze bartendaire." So Carlo Moglio and his wife Henriette also became friends.

Two weeks before returning home to America, we dined at the Grill. Carlo explained that while he was an excellent cook and had wanted to have us to their home for dinner, Henriette would have none of it because, as he put it, "We live in the slums."

I reassured Carlo that we didn't care, to which he replied that, had he known, he would have invited us over sooner. I said, "We have two more weeks here. When shall we come?"

The following Monday night, following Carlo's directions, we arrived on the bus. He met us on the corner, cosh (a billy club) in hand, and led us to a decrepit brick row house. On the second floor, he opened the door onto a room that would have pleased the Count of Monte Cristo: Aubusson carpet, gilded Louis XV chairs with

Fragonard-style tapestry seats, and a large crystal chandelier. The seven-course meal was memorable, with foie gras and cheeses that had arrived from France that morning. After dinner, a Spanish couple arrived in full flamenco regalia. He played the guitar while she danced for us.

After the performance, I confessed to Carlo my curiosity about his past. Carlo responded, "Our life in Paris became too expensive; so we moved to London, where we have the choice of living poorly in a swell section of town or beautifully in a poor section."

Following our return to the states, from the time I was twenty-seven until I turned fifty, I worked at my father's factory, all the while diving into the arts and the environment, building my portfolio of useful "products." In college, I had majored in English. After flunking chemistry, trigonometry, and calculus, I took one semester of accounting because it was absolutely clear that I couldn't deal with numbers. And yet, I subsequently ran a large, successful manufacturing, sales, and services corporation.

How did I do it? I learned from other people by acknowledging their expertise and accepting their help. When I didn't understand chemistry, I hired a chemist. When I couldn't handle finances, I hired a financial expert. When I realized I wasn't an effective administrator, I employed two excellent administrators. It was largely my contacts, combined with my curiosity and imagination, that allowed me, with the help of several hundred employees, to run a successful textiles business. In more than twenty-five years at the company, I am proud to say I never once laid off an employee, nor did we ever have a union problem during my tenure.

When I was made president at age thirty, I joined the Young Presidents Organization (YPO). Membership required presidency of a fairly sizeable firm before age forty and retirement by age fifty. Thanks to my fellow members I learned about mergers and acquisitions and, during this period, added several complementary businesses to our company, necessitating a name change to Hanes Companies.

My first marriage to the wonderful Joan Humpstone was highlighted by travel and involvement in the arts and lasted thirty-three years. After her death, I married another wonderful woman, Charlotte Metz, who is interested in the outdoors, animals, people, and is committed to serving others. Both relationships have given me emotional stability and the experience of a deep-seated joy in the glories of a solid marriage and a harmonious home life.

Somewhere along the way, I found my real source of strength in the knowledge, the presence, the support, and the love and respect of the Lord and his only Son. At the age of seventy-five, I resolved that my next ten years would be my most productive. True to my conviction, I can honestly tell you I am busier now than I have ever been in my life. What a tragedy it is when highly capable men and women retire from life instead of using their experience, talents, skills, financial resources and other gifts from the Almighty to help others make a go of their lives. Sharing some of the pleasures I enjoy with those who may not be able to afford them is certainly one of my greatest joys.

Although the notion of civic duty is not particularly American, Americans see their civic duty in a very particular light: everyone has a civic duty, but no one is compelled to perform it. It is the obligation we undertake in gratitude for the rights we enjoy. But the idea of obligation is not especially popular. We hear far more about individual rights.

In the pages that follow, I offer some of the "wares" I have acquired in the belief they will be helpful to you and in your endeavors. My wares are Networking, Risk-Taking, Fund-Raising, and Problem-Solving. They can, I believe, show you how to get anyone to do anything. I hope you will find them useful. But I also hope you will use them for good purposes.

YOU CAN ACCOMPLISH ANYTHING
■ YOU CAN DREAM—IF YOU CAN FIND ■
SOMEONE ELSE TO DO IT.

This is the basic premise of this book—persuading others to accomplish your goals. This is indeed, outsourcing, if you like. It works because the "someone else" are those who will benefit from the result and who will get the credit for achievement. My part is to identify the project, indicate the path to follow, empower the participants, and remove obstacles that might impede progress.

The four parts of this book—Networking, Risk-Taking, Fund-Raising, and Problem-Solving—are rather arbitrary divisions, but useful. I see them like the four suits in a deck of cards. In a hand of bridge, each card can be valuable in combination with others in the same suit, or it can add value to the usefulness of techniques and concepts in another suit. If your goal is a complex one, you will need several players. Thus, for example, if you hope to raise operating or capital funds for a national organization or corporation, networking and fund-raising techniques should be used in tandem.

Although I use the stories that follow to illustrate one particular technique or another, you will find that often I use more than one technique in the context of a single project. My stories are not precise blueprints, and the goals they describe are infinitely varied. Each reader must substitute his or her own goals for mine. I once infuriated Leonard Bernstein when I referred to him as "the world's greatest salesman for good music."

"I am no salesman!" he expostulated, "I just try to educate the uninformed."

Well, to me a teacher is a salesman of ideas and concepts, someone who persuades someone else to learn. After all, is there really much difference between raising money for a church and selling tickets for a symphony benefit? Both institutions seek to elevate the mind, the spirit, and the soul. The salesman who goes from door to door has the same mission as the Seventh-Day Adventist who goes from door to door: both will find the techniques I describe relevant and useful. So use your imagination and re-word my text and adapt my techniques to suit the project at hand. I doubt, however, whether any single technique or anecdote will provide all the answers. This book should be more of a stimulant to the imagination than a step-by-step workbook.

One of my recurring pleasures is to sit down with a small group of people, listen to them describe their projects and goals, and then help them lay out some plan to implement them. However, I believe this book will be useful only to those whose motives are good. If you are going to be the sole beneficiary, you may find it difficult to interest others in your cause. My own guide in this respect has been a wise and wonderful book entitled *God Calling*, edited by A.J. Russell and published by Dodd & Mead. In print for more than twenty-five years, I have given copies to dozens of people and still refer to it almost daily. Invariably, I find it answers my questions and addresses my concerns.

PART 1

NETWORKING

*Stand on someone's shoulders. You can travel farther carried
on the accomplishments of those who came before you.
And the view is much better*

—BRUCE MAU, "An Incomplete Manifesto
for Growth"

Networking, according to Webster's Collegiate Dictionary 11th Edition: "The exchange of information or services among individuals, groups, or institutions; the cultivation of productive relationships for employment or business." But this is as simplistic as the definition of the card game bridge as: "A game in which one partnership plays to fulfill certain declarations against opponents acting as defenders."

In practical terms, if you wish to network creatively, you must have more than names and telephone numbers in a Rolodex, address book, computer. You need useful information as well. I use a Palm Pilot and with it I can cross-reference any number of relevant pieces of information about each contact I make, including:

Name: _____

Relationships: married/single/children/pets, etc.

Location: New York, San Francisco, London

Business/profession: doctor/plastic surgeon

Other skills: marketing, promotion, public relations, fund-raising

Hobbies/interests: gardening (horticulture/orchids), cooking, wine, painting (watercolors), flying, cycling

Affiliations: clubs/charities/religious

Think about the requirements of your own projects and then set up relevant and useful categories that you add to each listing whenever you add a new name. This may seem tedious at first, but you'd be surprised how quickly you'll see the bigger picture coming into focus once you begin adding notes to the names of friends and acquaintances. For example, if I am to entertain an out-of-town visitor whom I'd like to involve in one of my projects, I would consider inviting one additional dinner guest for each of my visitor's special interests. If these additional guests are good friends, I would ask them to help me engage with and educate the visitor on the value of my project. If I can help my visitor feel comfortable, feel like he or she "is one of us," they are far more likely to support my cause.

I came across a fascinating story in *The New Yorker* (January 11, 1999) entitled "Six Degrees of Lois Weisberg." Lois Weisberg of Chicago had "done hundreds of things in her life and met thousands of people" and enjoyed recruiting people into "one of her grand schemes." She seemed to know everybody. She's just one of those people, according to Malcolm Gladwell, the author of the article, who "spread ideas and information. They connect varied and isolated parts of society. . . . Lois is a connector." One of her friends observed that she "doesn't network just for the sake of networking." She simply tries to connect with people and help them connect with one another. She "knows a lot of people" and "belongs to lots of different worlds."

Mark Granovetter, one of the researchers cited in the article, confirms what we already understand—that knowing a lot of people can be of practical as well as emotional support. For instance, someone with whom we are connected, whether the connections are strong or weak, close or distant, can help us find a new job, or obtain new information, or expose us to new ideas. In fact, Granovetter believes in what he calls "the strength of weak ties." That is, even people you know who are not close to you can be of help to you.

Strong ties or tenuous ones, connections lead to networking. And connections can be the key to getting anybody to do anything. And that suggests there are no such things as weak ties.

N^o CHANCE MEETINGS

*The Lord shall preserve thy going out and thy coming
in from this time forth, and even evermore.*

—PSALM 12:8

My life continues to be full of adventure and new experiences, and I believe that all events hold significance and all chance meetings have potential importance. To illustrate this, let me tell you of a day a few months ago when many good things came together at once.

The Southeastern Center of Contemporary Arts (SECCA) in Winston-Salem—a gallery that offers exhibition space and makes sales for the work of local artists—sponsored an international competition for architects to design affordable two- and three-bedroom houses, based on the Habitat for Humanity format, for low-income families. The homes would also be "green" houses, that is, designed to be energy efficient and built using environmentally sustainable materials. The Forsyth County Technical Community College in

Winston-Salem agreed to test all the new materials and provide students to build some of the houses. More than four hundred designs were submitted and exhibited, and the Winston-Salem Housing Partnership (a nonprofit agency that builds low-income housing on land that it owns) elected to build the first structure.

I knew right away that this had the potential to become a pilot project for a national program. We had three important players in place: SECCA, to generate the interest and provide the workable blueprints; the Housing Partnership, to provide a building site and possibly some funding; and the community college, to test the materials and train young builders in new concepts and techniques.

I suggested we contact Neal Peirce, a syndicated columnist for the *Washington Post* and one of America's leading reporters on governmental/legislative affairs and ask him to report on the project. I then suggested that we put our plans before the Department of Housing and Urban Development (HUD) for support.

On November 19, 2003, the entire project came together in a succession of meetings and phone calls that was gratifying in its results and quite remarkable in its timing. At 7:30 A.M. I had breakfast with Gary Green, the president of the technical college, to discuss the project.

At 10:00 A.M. Selwa Roosevelt, President Reagan's chief of protocol and a personal friend, called from Washington, D.C., to tell me about her dinner for Dana Gioia, the chairman of the National

Endowment for the Arts. When I brought up the housing plan, she immediately offered to introduce us to Mel Martinez, the director of HUD.

At 11:00 A.M. David Brown of SECCA called to say that Neal Peirce wanted to discuss the project with me.

At 12:30 P.M. I called Angelos Angelou, of Angelou Economics in Austin, Texas, a consulting firm that was producing a study to revitalize eight counties in northwestern North Carolina, including ours. I suggested that the SECCA project could be an exemplary demonstration of Winston-Salem's ability to produce design work with a national application. Angelou told me that Henry Cisneros, the former director of HUD, was now the chief executive officer of KB Houses, the largest builders of low- to moderate-income housing in the United States. Angelos said that, according to Cisneros, HUD had wanted to get involved.

At 4:00 P.M. Neal Peirce called to say that he was indeed writing an article.

At 6:30 P.M. I talked to Bill Benton, a local builder of low-income retirement homes, who agreed to fill in some technical details on the program.

Shortly after Neal Peirce's article appeared in the *Washington Post* and elsewhere, the Smithsonian Institution asked SECCA if it might use the competition entries as the centerpiece for a forthcoming exhibition of designs for low-cost housing. Bill Benton is planning to build seven of the houses in Winston-Salem, and we seem to have sowed the seeds of a program that could do much to encourage the growth of low-income housing across the country. In the space of a single day we had tapped into several sources for raising funds and approaches to finding expertise. To me, such events are small miracles of encouragement. Others call them coincidences. My Jewish friends say "b'sherritt (it was meant to be)."

EVERYBODY KNOWS

In 1963, Terry Sanford, the governor of North Carolina, offered to establish a conservatory for the performing arts in any city in North Carolina that could provide dormitory space and classrooms for four hundred students. If these facilities were donated, the state would pick up the operating costs and add this school to the greater University of North Carolina system. Each city would have to raise $1 million to match an equal amount from the Ford Foundation.

In response—after all, the city that called itself the City of the Arts should certainly be the home of its state art school—our mayor formed the Winston-Salem Conservatory Investigation Committee. The members included Charles Babcock Jr., of the Babcock Foundation, Mrs. Agnew Bahnson Jr., a founder of the Arts Council, M. C. Benton Jr., the mayor, Mrs. Winfield Blackwell, president of the Arts Council, Dr. Dale Gramley, president of Salem College, James A. Gray, president of Old Salem, Inc., devoted to historic preservation, Bill Herring, executive director of the Arts Council, Jim Rush, editor at the *Winston-Salem Journal and Sentinel,* Sebastian Sommer of the Winston-Salem Foundation, Ralph Stockton, chairman of the trustees of Winston-Salem State College, and Dr. Harold Tribble, president of Wake Forest College (now Wake Forest University). I was the chairman.

The site we selected for our bid was the former Forsyth Hospital in East Winston. Unfortunately, the governor liked this building so well that he chose it for another school that he was introducing to the state, the North Carolina Advancement School for Under-Achievers, to be headed up by Peter Buttenwieser of Philadelphia. Thus we were left without a site and no ideas for a substitute.

While we were looking around for a new site, the author John Ehle, who was also the governor's assistant, told me that Sanford was planning to start a summer school for gifted children and was going to locate it at Meredith College in Raleigh. I asked if we could bid for it. John said, "Well, the governor has not told Meredith anything about this, so of course you can." I immediately called Dr. Gramley and Jim Gray and the two of them put together a committee that secured for Winston-Salem and Salem College the first Governor's School for Gifted Children in the United States. Since then virtually every state in the nation has established such a school.

Winston-Salem had become the home of two unique state schools, but we still had our eyes on the proposed North Carolina School for the Arts. Two or three weeks before the final decision on the location for the conservatory, Marvin Ward, the superintendent of Winston-Salem/Forsyth County Schools, told me that the school system had decided to abandon Gray High School and asked if we could use the building. We jumped on it, and secured the services of architect Nils Larsen. A new mandate required that we provide classrooms and dormitories for only two hundred students with the state providing future funding. We persuaded Larsen to give us a plan and a price estimate, a process that occupied ten of the fourteen days before the governor's committee was scheduled to visit each of the applicants and decide on the school's location.

Using an early computer called the McBee Keysort, Bill Herring, a former director of the Arts Council, and I went through the list of donors to the council and its member groups and put together a fund-raising campaign committee. We had no idea how much money to raise, or quite how we'd do it on such short notice. We didn't realize it, but we were depending on a local network of individuals to provide the results we rather vaguely envisioned.

Shortly afterward Ruth Julian, a local patron of the arts, invited my wife Joan and me to dine with her, her husband Ira, and Smith Bagley of the Z. Smith Reynolds Foundation. We talked about the challenge of raising $1 million (the equivalent of $5 million in today's dollars) in a few days. Smith said, "Why don't we raise the money on the telephone?"

I started to say, "Everybody knows you can't raise that kind of money over the telephone!" Then I remembered that, buried inside the phrase "everybody knows you can't _____," there's always a glorious opportunity.

It's exciting to see how a network (noun) can network (verb). Once it's set in motion, it expands and regenerates itself. Wallace Carroll, who was editor-in-chief of the Winston-Salem paper, oversaw articles in the need for the school and the toughness of the competition. He even ran two long front-page editorials while we were putting together the campaign.

Several large businesses in town pledged their support if we could prove that the community really wanted a conservatory. Bill Herring and I and our associates organized a phone campaign in two days. After only twenty-four hours of fund-raising, we had $1 million. Over five thousand donors gave a total in excess of $825,000; community foundations and local corporations provided the rest.

The governor convened a review committee of major figures in the performing arts, including the choreographer Agnes de Mille, the dancer José Limón, and the playwrights Paul Green and Richard Adler. They visited our site and then walked through the Arts Council and the Chamber of Commerce. Many of these visiting artists had tears in their eyes as they saw our network in action.

Several other cities in North Carolina promoted various locations, promising, "Give us the conservatory and we will raise the money." Winston-Salem said, "We want the conservatory and believe so passionately that it should be here, we have already raised the money." We got the conservatory, hands down.

IT'S NOT WHAT YOU KNOW

After turning over the role of chief executive officer of Hanes Companies to a successor in 1976, I founded Ampersand, a consulting company for nonprofit organizations, with a special interest in those concerned with the arts. One of our early commissions came from the Wake Forest University School of Medicine, which wanted to raise $400,000 from the Kresge Foundation in Birmingham, Michigan. Our research indicated that Kresge's review process was one of the nation's most rigorous and that almost routinely the foundation would fund only half of a grant request. So we advised our clients to double the request to $800,000 and develop meticulous supporting documentation. Further information gleaned from past Kresge recipients told us that once a request made it past the lions at the gate, personal acquaintance with board and staff could assure success.

In *Who's Who in America*, I learned that the president of the foundation, Bill Baldwin, had graduated from the University of Michigan at about the same time as my friend Ralph Getsinger. A call to Ralph was a triumph. Baldwin had been his roommate. Further research revealed that the vice president of the foundation was

Ted Taylor, whose mother lived in Asheville, North Carolina; whenever Ted visited her, he enjoyed hiking with my friend Jamie Clark. Armed with these connections, I set up the visit.

In the meantime, the Ketchum Company, a prominent fund-raising organization, had been engaged to run the campaign. Ketchum believed that those of us at Ampersand were out of our minds and that our advice was absurd. According to Ketchum, the Kresge Foundation and Duke Endowment (a huge fund dedicated primarily to supporting health care, universities, and churches in North Carolina) were close associates. When representatives of Kresge made site visits to the South, they often used the Endowment offices as their headquarters. Duke had just granted Wake $400,000, and for us to suggest that Wake ask Kresge for twice that amount was sheer folly. Kresge would surely find out about the Duke grant and feel perfectly justified in refusing even to consider as large a sum.

My response, "We know what we're doing and are willing to risk our reputation on it."

Ralph Getsinger gave a dinner for us and invited the Baldwins and another friend (and member of Kresge's board), Ed Lerchen, and his wife. The Getsingers, Baldwins, and Lerchens would be vacationing together in Europe the week after the Kresge Foundation had made its funding decisions. Over cocktails before dinner, I said that I understood that Baldwin had been involved in the Nuremberg trials of German war criminals, which prompted an interesting discussion. I then observed that Michigan remained cool much of the year, which meant that one could play paddle tennis longer than would have been comfortable in the South.

"You like paddle tennis!" he exclaimed. "I'll bet you didn't know that I founded the Lone Pine Paddle Tennis Club, the first one in Michigan!" By then we were really enjoying each other's company. This was not difficult, because he was a fascinating man.

"I understand from Ralph that you and your friends are calling on Kresge tomorrow," Baldwin said. I told him that, as Ted Taylor was familiar with the state of North Carolina, we had submitted the request to him.

"Well," he said. "I'm sure Ed and I would like to hear about it. Why don't we step out on the porch for a moment and check it out?"

The next morning at Kresge, I joined Dick Janeway, the president of the Wake Forest University Medical School, John Watlington, the chief executive officer of Wachovia Bank, and Albert Butler, the president of Arista Industries and the chairman of the medical school board. On the trip home, we all agreed the meeting had gone well. One member of the group suggested the best we could count on was half of what Duke had given, $200,000; another thought we'd get $400,000. In fact, we received the entire $800,000.

This is not a singular experience. You will find that diligent research on personalities and interests combined with a meticulously developed request is critical to success. In almost all of my activities, contacts count. So often it is not what you know, but who. In this case, Ralph Getsinger was the "who."

THE BOYS IN THE BACK ROOM

The stories that follow are about two people who were in unlikely positions to provide major assistance, but who could —and did—proving that who you know doesn't necessarily have to be listed in *Who's Who* to be helpful to you.

My cousins owned Chatham Manufacturing Company, maker of blankets, furniture, and auto upholstery. Their major automotive customer, General Motors (also serviced by three competing upholstery suppliers), was never easy to work with. Each year, GM's purchasing agent would estimate the materials required and then say, "Of course, depending on seasonal sales, this can be plus or minus 15 percent."

Upholstery fabrics are laborious to produce, requiring lots of machine time, and the yarns must be ordered months in advance. In this business, the difference between a bust or bonanza in any given year depended on the quality of the tea leaves one was given to read or the correct toss of a coin. If only, said my cousins, there were better ways of predicting advance automobile sales.

In the mid-1950s, Chatham sales agent, Ralph Getsinger, found his tea leaf reader when he learned that Matt Badlimenti, in GM's back office, was a wiz with a calculator. It was to Matt that the GM purchasing agent went for his final report before placing orders with the suppliers. And Matt had figured out the requirements months earlier.

Matt was a delightful man to know. I was privileged to go with the Chatham Manufacturing entourage to football games in Detroit and often sat with Matt on the fifty-yard line. Matt was greatly appreciative of the steak and wine dinners that followed. And Chatham Manufacturing was no less appreciative of his "ideas" about GM's future upholstery needs.

When President Johnson appointed me to the National Council of the Arts in 1965, I was the only businessman and the only Southerner in the company of such luminaries as Isaac Stern, Leonard Bernstein, John Steinbeck, Agnes de Mille, and Helen Hayes, among others. I knew, however, that the support staff remain long after the celebrity appointees' terms expire, so I set about making friends with staff. I always gave my government per diem to the dining room to provide them with dinner wine.

The National Endowment for the Arts was created the following year, which provided funding for National Council programs. A program director was chosen for each discipline (such as dance, drama, music, literature, etc.). Money was allocated, in part, by the programs that garnered the most national attention, and thus the approval of key congressmen.

I saw that the key ingredient for grant requests by the organizations I wished to help would be accurate, detailed, and timely information. Florence Lowe, the incredibly able director of public relations for the NEA, was privy to everything. Each program director told her whatever she wished to know in the hope that his or her program would receive the most press.

She became my much beloved and courted Yiddisher mama. As a result she helped me with three $500,000 challenge grants, at least one of which would never have gotten to the first cut without her assistance. Like Matt, she didn't need to be in *Who's Who* to be influential.

So don't just look at the front office of an organization for the assistance you need with a project. Sometimes you'll discover your most capable help sits in the back room.

HOLDING THE COURSE

It takes many years to become an overnight success.

—ANON

During a storm at sea, it is difficult to maintain a true compass course. So it is when attempting to reach a long-term goal. But the results are often worth the effort.

In 1962, while I was president of the Arts Councils of America, Roger L. Stevens was appointed by President Kennedy to replace Corrin Strong at the floundering National Cultural Center (now the Kennedy Center). To raise funds, Roger organized a closed-circuit television broadcast that would showcase the performing arts in America. His program would constitute the entertainment during a series of dinners across the country. Sponsored by local symphonies and arts councils, the dinners were priced at $100 a person, with the profits to be split between the sponsors and the NCC before the hosting arts council paid for the meal. I advised the arts councils to forget it.

Roger was furious and sent a mutual friend, Selwa Roosevelt, to straighten me out. When she returned she told Roger that I had acted correctly for my constituency: I maintained that, other than making a publicity blip, the project would do little to raise funds. Furthermore, Selwa told Roger that if I were proven right, he should ask President Kennedy to appoint me to the NCC's board. A few weeks later, I became a board member of the National Cultural Center.

Following my first board meeting in New York, my wife and I accepted an invitation to Roger's apartment in the Carlyle. "Come meet a few of your fellow board members," Roger said. Later that evening, after refilling my wine glass, Roger invited me to see his library. On entering, he closed the double doors behind us.

"How dare you sabotage a funding drive for the nation's performing arts center?" he began, and lit into me with a vengeance.

When I did not back down, Roger laughed and said that it was unusual for any of his associates to stand up to him. "I need that occasionally," he said. "I think you and I will be friends." At that moment, my life was changed forever.

Through my friendship with Roger, opportunities to serve the nation's arts scene came like a flood. Appointed by President Kennedy to the National Cultural Center in 1962, I was reappointed by President Ford in 1975. Roger sponsored my membership to America's oldest and most important arts clubs, the Century in

New York, and the Bohemian Club in San Francisco. In fact, it was largely through Roger's mentorship that I became a networker.

That said, I do not mean to imply that you should always adhere to the already proven ways of doing things. The world is in a state of constant change, and we must keep a weather eye on new ideas and innovations. Buckminster Fuller wrote in my holographic book, "In the evolution of political man of the late twentieth century, there is an emerging pattern in which yesterday's vices become tomorrow's virtues and, vice versa, virtues vices."

The past success of a steady course does not mean that one should not change it in order to catch a favorable wind or avoid a dangerous shoal.

EVERYONE LOVES A PARTY

People involved in business, the arts, the environment, education, and other fields usually welcome the chance to be with one another socially—especially if the occasion differs from the usual format of a conference or convention. When planning an event, the trick is to build a core list of people whom you have a reasonable chance of attracting. When you have succeeded with most of these, then build the rest of the gathering by citing the names of those who have already accepted.

The South Eastern Center of Contemporary Art in Winston-Salem had an interesting idea that illustrates this ploy. In 1981, SECCA initiated a new regional program, called the Southeast Seven, to expose seven regional artists to a national audience. I arranged for Piedmont Airlines (now US Airways) to loan us a plane and provide our guests with complimentary round trips from New York City and Washington, D.C. We assembled a world-class guest list of museum patrons and art collectors: from New York, representing the Museum of Modern Art, Mrs. John D. Rockefeller; Bill Lieberman and Henry Geldzahler of the Metropolitan Museum of Art, and Seymour Knox of the Albright/Knox Gallery in Buffalo.

From Washington were Nancy Hanks and Brian O'Doherty (also known as the sculptor Patrick Ireland) of the NEA, and Josh Taylor of the National Museum of American Art (now the Smithsonian Institution Museum of American Art). Other guests included Sydney and Frances Lewis (Virginia Museum of Art), Mrs. P. R. Norman (Museum of Contemporary Art, New Orleans), Jim and Marilyn Alsdorf (Art Institute of Chicago) and Ben Williams, director of the North Carolina Museum of Art. And this formidable group gathered for nothing other than a chance to get together, be entertained, and chat with each other. The concept was unusual and eagerly embraced by all. The weekend was covered in Town and Country by Selwa Roosevelt (who subsequently became President Reagan's chief of protocol). Winston-Salem still uses reprints of her article when publicizing the cultural life of the city—if only to point out progress since then!

This party was launched when the plane lost power outside Washington and had to return to the airport. Henry Geldzahler, sitting with Brian O'Doherty, remarked, "My God! What a tragedy! I can see tomorrow's headlines, 'Plane carrying Blanchette Rockefeller, Seymour Knox, Nancy Hanks, and others crashes.' I have never been an 'other' in my whole career."

This event only heightened the group's exuberance. And the weekend was a huge success. Great things followed, all made easier because the movers and shakers in the art world were now familiar with SECCA's high standards. At that exhibition, Josh Taylor of the Smithsonian agreed to purchase at least one work for his museum's permanent collection. He chose the work of Irwin Kremen, and SECCA gave him a one-man show. This was Kremen's very first public exhibition and from it he immediately earned his first national exhibition in the Smithsonian American Art Museum. He is now internationally recognized and in 2001 held his third exhibition in Japan. In 1981, when SECCA wanted to establish a major new national program, the Awards in the Visual Arts, I was able to get Howard Klein, the director of arts programs for the Rockefeller Foundation, and Nancy Hanks, the chairman of the National Endowment for the Arts, to fund and support it. Nancy brought in Coy Ecklund, the president of Equitable Life Insurance as the third partner.

Over the years, SECCA has had good relationships and valuable exposure in many of the museums represented at that unforgettable weekend party. When your business or organization has something with lasting consequences it wishes to promote, there are few better ways to do this than to gather together the leadership in the field and give them a memorable event that will be appreciated long after it occurs. If Winston-Salem, then a city of about 150,000 people, could do it, your city can too.

USS ZELLARS DD777

In 1951, during the Korean War, the navy recalled me for service on a destroyer that, having just finished an over-long tour of duty in Korea, was now stationed in the Atlantic. My eight months aboard before being sent abroad read like a sequel to Mr. Roberts. One episode fits here. On a night in the North Atlantic in hurricane conditions surrounded by icebergs, two large supply ships in our flotilla collided, sheering off their bows. One seaman was killed. Our destroyer and one other were selected to lead the supply ships into Halifax, Nova Scotia, at five knots. We took a horrendous beating in that storm, losing all of our stanchions and the two-inch-thick steel flying bridge.

On reaching port, Captain Hayes said, "Hanes, you'll be the first man ashore. Get another officer and rent a furnished house, get a good caterer, and a woman for every officer. We are going to have a party tomorrow night."

"But, Sir," I said, "I have never been to Halifax."

"What's that to me? Get going. That's an order."

I selected another ensign and said to him, "You find the house and I'll find the ladies and the caterer." I looked in the phone book and found that Halifax had a Junior League. When I explained, with a few embellishments, the horrors we'd faced and pointed out the uniqueness of our crew—"the captain and gunnery officer are Annapolis (true) and the balance are grads of Ivy League colleges (a considerable exaggeration)"—I had her attention. "Whilst (I used the English version to make a good impression) we are here we would much enjoy meeting some of the fine ladies of Halifax. We are renting a lovely home for the evening and would appreciate it if you could also advise us of the best caterer in town. Libations and dinner will be at seven."

We had a wonderful evening and found that Halifax ladies were delightful and very empathetic when we told them of our travails.

WILLIE SUTTON HAD IT RIGHT

he New Testament suggests that the meek shall inherit the earth. Well, that's fine if that's what you want. But meekness is not a very good idea if you are running for Congress, or trying to raise money, or planning on building an organization or company with more than local assistance. The impresario, Sol Hurok, who first brought Russian opera and ballet to the United States, had to make his name famous to achieve his mission. In an address to the American Symphony Orchestra League, he claimed, "Of all the famous people I have met, I am the most humble." Humble he was not, nor does humility pay when you wish to achieve more ambitious goals.

Some years after helping to found the Winston-Salem Arts Council, the first arts council in the United States, I told its director I wanted to make Winston-Salem the cultural capital of the South. His response, "You can't do it by sitting here in town." Thus it was he helped me join my first national board, the American Symphony Orchestra League, in 1956. And thus began my long career of being the "token Southerner" on regional and national boards around the country. I'm often asked why I spent so much time on boards that had no apparent involvement in Winston-Salem. "For the same reason," I say, "that Willie Sutton became the world's greatest bank robber. His jailer asked why he kept on robbing banks when he nearly always got caught. Willie answered, 'You fool, that's where the money is.'"

National boards choose their members based on power, prestige, and/or resources. To bring the benefits of those attributes home, you have to be willing to work on their committees and do a better-than-average job. Many board members assume they were chosen for their wisdom rather than their ability to give or get, and lack the wisdom to get out. Thus the motto of a good board: Give, get, or get out.

Because I served on so many national boards, in 1956 I was appointed by President Johnson to the first board of the National Council of the Arts (the advisory body to the NEA), at the suggestion of Roger Stevens, chairman of the NEA. When later I formed the Board of Visitors for the North Carolina School of the Arts, I was able to persuade Roger to be its chairman and choreographer Agnes de Mille, actress Helen Hayes, set designer Oliver Smith, and dancer Edward Villella to sit on the board.

When, at my instigation, the School of the Arts dedicated its fabulous fourteen-hundred-seat performance hall to Roger Stevens, I arranged the opening performance. Gregory Peck was master of ceremonies. Performing were Sir Anton Dolin, Jean Stapleton, Helen Hayes, Rosemary Harris, Cliff Robertson, Mel Tomlinson, and Heather Watts (who danced the pas de deux from New York City

Ballet's *Agon*). With Isaac Stern as the soloist, Leonard Bernstein conducted the NCSA student orchestra in Mendelssohn's Violin Concerto in E minor. All the performers participated without pay.

When the South Eastern Center for Contemporary Art (SECCA) decided to establish an advisory board, I was able to invite Joe Hirschhorn to become chairman, and Sydney and Frances Lewis and the art critic Dorothy Miller to join the board. None of this would have been possible without years of building contacts while serving on national boards. I attribute my wide-ranging approaches in great part to my contacts—my network.

Nothing is more satisfying than serving your community, state, and country. Even more exciting is to do so in many different capacities in widely varying organizations where you'll be exposed to many different people who are, themselves, dealing with a wide diversity of challenges and opportunities. A truly good performance will assure additional invitations to join other boards. And it's not all hard work. Your understanding and ability to operate in many fields of endeavor, amidst the security of numerous and diverse friendships, provides a deep-seated personal pleasure.

Now, at the age of seventy-nine, I can envision a time when I might wish to relax and join the rose-sniffing society. Thanks to my huge roster of friends and contacts, I know I won't suffer even a minute's-worth of loneliness or boredom.

PART 2

RISK-TAKING

Begin anywhere. John Cage tells us that not knowing where to begin is a common form of paralysis. His advice: Begin anywhere.

—BRUCE MAU, "An Incomplete Manifesto for Growth"

When faced with a project, develop a manageable little chart that puts your plan into an ordered sequence of events with dates and time of accomplishment noted. Then populate the project with the appropriate people. Don't be bashful. It doesn't hurt to ask someone to get involved.

I'm reminded of the time when, as a young salesman, I had to approach my first potential client. Much of our business involved the dyeing and finishing of clothing interlinings—pockets, waistbands, and so on. The low-end clothing district in New York was about as foreign to me as Marrakech or Mauritania. I was, frankly, terrified.

The head of our New York office gave me some pointers in a brief scenario. "Ask yourself," he suggested, "Where am I? I'm out here. Where is the prospective buyer? He's in there. Where should I be? In there. Suppose he throws me out, where will I be? Out here. Where am I now? So what have I got to lose?"

Many years later, I had the perfect opportunity to apply his suggestion. On a flight from Pittsburgh to Greensboro, I was joined by a friend of many years, the ceramic artist Cynthia Bringle, who lives and works at the Penland School for Crafts in the Blue Ridge Mountains. She told me about what was reputed to be the world's largest teapot collection, amounting to several thousand examples. She also said that approximately 250 of the teapots were part of a traveling exhibition, that went to Toronto, Napa and Long Beach in California, Chicago, and Charlotte, attracting record crowds and national media attention. She also told me that the collectors, Solomon and Gloria Kamm, had made it known they wanted to find a home for their collection somewhere in the South, in a city where it would be the major attraction, and where its presence would have a beneficial financial impact. I knew exactly where it should go.

The next day, I called Mr. Kamm and said I had learned of his world famous teapot collection and knew he wished to have it exhibited in the South and I had the perfect location for him— Sparta, North Carolina.

"Where's that?" he asked.

I told him Sparta was a delightful little spot with a population of about twelve hundred people.

"Oh no! " he responded. "That's way too small!"

Then I began my pitch, "Well, Mr. Kamm, listen to this. Number one: Since the nation's second 'tea party' was in Eden, North Carolina (it followed Boston's famous event a year later), North Carolina is where the museum should be. And you want it in a location where it will have an important economic impact."

"It will surely do that in such a tiny town," he interrupted.

I continued, "Number two: Sparta is ten minutes from the Blue Ridge Parkway, which in 2003 attracted more than 22 million visitors from all over the United States and Europe. Your museum in Sparta would attract a percentage of those visitors, say 150,000 people.

"Number three: The parkway advertises a craft corridor that runs from the Virginia border to Asheville. The closest crafts venue to Virginia is the Northwest Trading Post, forty-one miles down the road. Your museum would be the northern anchor of the entire corridor.

"Number four: Sparta is central to four counties that straddle the Blue Ridge Parkway. Unemployment in three of those counties hovers at plus or minus 10 percent. The financial impact from tourism, people building summer homes, and an influx of small businesses could be significant in this region of impoverished Appalachia."

Before that conversation, I had not met Solomon Kamm nor heard of his teapots. But that cold call was successful in bringing his collection to Sparta.

When a worthwhile idea presents itself, go ahead and take a shot at it. You never can tell where what you read in the tea leaves might lead you. The key is to prepare yourself thoroughly before you start a project. As they say in Sparta, "Measure twice, cut once."

ANYTHING WORTH DOING
IS WORTH DOING POORLY

Drift. Allow yourself to wander aimlessly.

Explore adjacencies.

Lack judgment.

Postpone criticism.

—BRUCE MAU, "An Incomplete Manifesto
for Growth"

This is not an excuse for shoddy work; it merely suggests that perfectionism isn't always that useful. A good place to start anything [a book or a job] is at the beginning. But, how to start? Nothing is more daunting than that first step, that first page. The artist Jasper Johns said about sculpture, "Take an object. Do something to it. Do something else to it." Or when faced with a blank canvas, "Take a canvas. Put a mark on it. Put another mark on it." Many people have good ideas, but they wait to dot every 'i' and cross every 't' and then, when it's time to implement the idea, they are either too bored to complete it or someone else has already done it. The plan that most creative and successful people tend to follow is to start the project and make corrections as they go along. Of course they make mistakes and often get criticism or worse, but as my young friend John Bryan, who shares my impatience, says, "Go for absolution rather than permission."

In 1978 I chaired the drive to convert the abandoned Carolina Theater and Hotel into a center for the performing arts in Winston-Salem. Before I could even put a committee together, the city's Contributions Council, which must approve any campaign seeking more than $500,000, revoked permission to raise the money in Winston-Salem. During the previous year, the Arts Council had already raised more than its annual goal of $1.5 million and did not believe that another campaign seeking $6 million was feasible. So, with some ad hoc associates, I visited Washington D.C. and raised $3,630,000 from five federal grant programs. Only then (because the grant money was contingent on the city's ability to complete the arts center) did I manage to obtain permission to raise the balance locally. I had never been to Washington looking for money; but as this was the only avenue open, I just did some research and went about doing the job. We actually raised over $6.5 million, but Mayor Corpening appropriated $3 million to build the Adams Mark Hotel (see page 53).

Equally unplanned, at least on my part, was my association with Sweet Potatoes. In 2002, two African-American women called on me when I was a commissioner at the Office of Cultural Affairs in Winston-Salem. They wanted to open the first restaurant in Winston's Art District, but the city had already turned them down twice and they had only one more opportunity to apply for a city loan. Their credentials were good: one had graduated from a culinary institute, had been apprenticed to the chef at the Deer Park Inn in County Cavan, Ireland, and worked currently as a sous chef in a retirement home. The other had eighteen years experience working in the front of the house at numerous restaurants.

I decided to give them a tryout and asked them to cater a crucial business dinner. The ladies did a first-class job for me. I then arranged an interview for them with a chef who had been involved with four prestigious restaurants and currently owned one of Winston's top restaurants. Next, I introduced them to the local small business association, which vetted, and approved, their business proposal. My associate and I then arranged a meeting with representatives of the Art District and the African-American community, who promised to dine at the restaurant and promote it. With the support we had managed to assemble, the women reapplied for and won their loan. Three years later, Sweet Potatoes was still at capacity every day for lunch and dinner, and as this book goes to press is 10- to 15-percent ahead of its business projection.

If something seems worth doing, take the idea and run with it, even if you cannot guarantee the outcome. Some projects, like these two examples, can be achieved in a few months or within a year. Many of my projects have taken many years to come to pass, well over ten years in some cases. And I have worked for more than fifty years on the revitalization of downtown Winston-Salem.

A man planting some oak seedlings was asked why he would do so when it would take the seedlings fifty years to be of any size; "after all, you are already fifty-five years old."

"Well, then," he said, "I had better hurry up!"

REACHING FOR THE MOON

B y way of introducing me to the auction houses in New York, my art history professor at Yale instructed me to "pick something desirable and bid on it." A first edition of Samuel Johnson's dictionary was offered with an estimate of $2,000. I bid $500. On the day of the auction there was a colossal snowstorm, the auction was sparsely attended, and I bought the dictionary. It now resides in the library at Salem College.

While still in college I coveted a portrait by Gilbert Stuart that was for sale at the Old Print Shop in New York. After visiting the gallery off and on over three years, gallery owner Harry Shaw Newman, informed me, "Your uncle (one of Mr. Shaw's best customers) wants me to help you get started collecting art. You've never even asked the price of this painting. It's cheap—the owner is asking only $12,000. Make me an offer. As you can see, I've had it more than three years and no one but you has shown any real interest."

That was in 1950 and I protested that I had just finished college and hadn't earned any money yet. But the gallery owner persisted. Finally, I said, "$5,000." He replied, "That's no offer!" Nevertheless, the following week my offer was accepted and I became the owner of Stuart's *Portrait of Miss Dick and Miss Forster*.

Sixteen years later, John Walker, director of the National Gallery, called to say that he understood that I had a double portrait by Gilbert Stuart. He asked if I would lend it to the museum for a major retrospective of Stuart's work. A few months later the *Washington Post* reviewed the exhibition in its magazine section, using my painting as the focal point and running the picture on the cover. In the catalogue, the painting was described as one of Stuart's very rare double portraits.

I asked for three different appraisals of the painting while it was on exhibit. The lowest was $250,000. Reaching for the moon had paid off. I decided that I now had $245,000 worth of mistakes I could make—and so began many years of collecting American art. Encouraged by this success, several years later I bid $5,000 for a bronze *FLAG* (one of three) by Jasper Johns that was being offered at $15,000. I won that bid also. A few years later it sold for $300,000.

When it came to collecting art, I had always been advised to reach for the most important works rather than for the second-tier pieces because the important ones increase both in market value and in your own eyes. Furthermore, if you buy only what you find it difficult to live without, you will always think you have made a good choice, even if the market seems to disagree with you. The market can, and probably will, change. So it's best not to buy with an eye to making a killing. People interested in that outcome will do better in the stock market.

> AS A LITTLE BOY I WANTED TO LOOK UNDER ROCKS, LOGS, ROOTS TO BE SURPRISED BY
> ■ A SNAKE, SALAMANDER, HELLGRAMMITE, OR ■ CRAWFISH. TODAY I PEEK UNDER STATEMENTS IN CONVERSATION TO EXTRACT SOME LITTLE ARROW POINTING TOWARD FURTHER AVAILABLE INSIGHTS.

When buying land, I have used a similar strategy. I buy only beautiful, undeveloped land just because that is what I love. Over the course of fifteen years I bought eleven hundred acres of land that is now the center of North Carolina's Stone Mountain Park. I purchased it for a net adjusted present value of $80,000 and gave it to the state for a tax break of $1,750,000. I could have sold it for even more.

I also acquired for our trout-fishing club a 9,300-acre portion of Mount Mitchell with perhaps the best trout stream in the United States. The net adjusted present value of the acquisition was about $1,700,000 after the eighteen years it took to acquire it. Some years later we donated the development rights for a tax deduction of $5,200,000, thus saving for posterity the view from the Blue Ridge Parkway. Soaring 6,680 feet, Mount Mitchell is the tallest mountain in the East. With a vertical drop of 3,700 feet, it exceeds that of Vail, Colorado, by 850 feet. And its ridge is a state park.

If there is a lesson to all this, I guess it would be that you usually do well if you try to do good; and you seldom make a mistake if you seek the highest quality. All you need is confidence. And confidence comes with practice.

THE WISDOM FROM FEAR

I have always had acrophobia. Wanting to overcome my fear of heights, I joined the Yale Outing Club and attended a mountain climbing event with other students from Princeton, Harvard, Dartmouth, Smith, Vassar, and Holyoke colleges. This was 1947, long before today's neat hooks, clamps, and loops were available. We were taught to use a climbing rope and nothing else!

The beginners' slope was just that. And after three trips, I was ready for the next challenge, a vertical cliff. But there were so many more intermediate climbers that a rank beginner like me was not wanted since I would only slow down the process.

So I went to the expert's cliff: 150 feet high with a seven-foot rounded ledge that protruded five feet beyond the cliff face. I watched as a cute coed jauntily wrapped her ropes, gathered herself into a ball, and projected herself backwards over the ledge. Singing all the while, she let the rope slip through her hands to the count of ten, just as we'd been instructed, and then swung in under the ledge before lowering herself to the ground. It all looked terribly easy. I watched her do this twice more. Gathering my courage in both hands, I approached the ledge and picked up the rope. The instructor asked me if I had experienced this type of cliff before.

"You don't think I'd be fool enough to try this for the first time do you?"

"Of course not," he said.

I adjusted the ropes and eased my way out to the edge. Then I looked over my shoulder at the rock-strewn bottom some 150 feet below. That was too much, one heck of a lot too much. Sheer panic set in. I went into hysterics and fell off the cliff. I had sense enough to release the rope; but when I grabbed it again, I saw that horrible rock ledge in my face. I flung my head back and just barely skidded in under it. Now I was completely horizontal. Slightly more tilt and the rope would come loose, giving my hands such a powerful yank that it would be impossible to maintain a grip. Inch by inch I lowered myself, laughing hysterically all the way down to the bottom. Finally, I felt the ground beneath me.

Up on top, gathered an audience of climbers had gathered. Thinking they were witnessing an amazing stunt, they were cheering and yelling "Encore!"

"Screw you!" I yelled back feebly, rolled up onto my hands and knees, crawled the quarter mile to my car, and headed back to Yale and a double martini, acrophobia intact.

A hero is no braver than an ordinary man, but he's braver five minutes longer.

—RALPH WALDO EMERSON

Next came my airplane. Surely, to peacefully soar over the landscape amidst the puffy clouds would make me more altitude tolerant. With my friend, Tag Montague, I purchased a Cessna 182, a lovely white plane with a green stripe down each side. It seated five, including the pilot. I had had the highest ground test scores of any other flying student that year. Frankly, it was raw fear that motivated me. I had practically memorized the course. And flying on sunny days in the spring held its own pleasures, especially when I soloed in a Piper Cub, cut off the engine, and drifted down to a landing while wobbling from side to side to dump air from the wings and thus slow down the forward motion.

There were mistakes, such as the time I landed on the small strip in Chapel Hill with a perfect touchdown at the front edge only to find myself using up almost the entire strip before managing to stop. "First time I ever seen a feller land here down wind," said the strip manager.

Then there was the reckoning. Mrs. Roger Milliken, chairwoman of the Spartanburg Arts Council, had asked me to address the members. On a typical (for those of us living at the foot of the mountains) summer day, I took off into a blue sky decorated with widely scattered thunderheads. As I neared the Hickory omni (a VHF directional radio beacon for aircraft), I was faced with a solid wall of clouds. Having no instrument flight rating, I took the wise course and turned around. But the thunderheads had now formed a phalanx behind me. I climbed to 15,000 feet and saw an opening ahead approximately where the Spartanburg airport should have been. Luckily, there it was, framed in a wreath of angry cumulus. I swooped down through the roughest air pockets you can imagine. Everything loose in the cabin took flight and all seemed to conspire to swat me in the face. I bounced to a shaky landing in front of the hanger. By the time the plane was tied down and I managed to reach shelter, a thunder and lightning storm tore into that airport with a fury only slightly shy of a hurricane and scared the hell out of me. It had all happened so fast. The next day I flew home, kicked the tires, and said to my friend Tag, "Sell that sucker!"

Lesson learned: There are all kinds of phobias. If you run into someone with ophidiaphobia, that person will probably always avoid snakes. Likewise, someone who worships money may have a phobia about fund-raisers. Decide when you are wasting your time.

THE RAP ROOM

In the 1970s, some of us in Winston-Salem became conscious of our city's racial divisions. In an attempt to improve this situation, the Arts Council came up with a project called the Rap Room, a space where people of both races might meet. One night the sculptor Clifford Earl and I decided to drop in after dinner. Two young African Americans were already in the room. When we introduced ourselves, one of them flicked open a six-inch switch blade, holding it about six inches from my stomach. Clifford held out his hand, saying, "My, what a beautiful knife. May I hold it?" With a bewildered expression, the young man handed it to him. Clifford opened and shut the blade a couple of times admiringly, closed it up, and handed it back. We chatted briefly for a few minutes and then left to dry out our pants.

OUR SON OF A BITCH

Be careful what you pray for. You might just get it.

I was made chief executive officer of Hanes Dye and Finishing Company at the age of thirty-eight. With virtually no business education and only one semester of accounting, it didn't take me long to realize that I needed help. Using the Activity Vector Analysis, a personality test I had learned to read, I found a fresh graduate from the University of North Carolina School of Business who seemed to be a self-made man. If there ever were a type-A personality, his was a triple A.

I shared his profile with the president and publisher of the company that published the AVA, who said I'd be damned lucky to hold onto the guy for even a year and, if I did, he would make my life miserable until he was promoted to CEO. The textile business was not for sissies, and we needed a really strong hand at the helm in the future. I knew I wanted to "train up" my own potential successor, rather than hire a head-hunter to find one when the time came.

After I hired him, this young man worked his way through the Springs Cotton Mill's training program and then our own program. He did stints in the New York sales office and assignments in our local office. He had not even finished his training when several employees reported his complaints about management's incompetence. Our vice president came to me several times and said, "I want to fire that S.O.B."

"No," I said. "We need an S.O.B. to help us run this company, and one day I want to make him *our* S.O.B."

Around this time I heard a talk by the president of another company, who asked his top young officers three questions:

1. What do you think of yourself and your abilities?

2. What do you think of my abilities as CEO?

3. Where do you want to be ten years from now?

I decided to put these questions to our young S.O.B. and I asked for his responses in writing.

"I am superbly suited for company leadership and I am not being afforded the opportunity to show off," he replied. He then asked to have complete control of my buffing wheel accounts (see page 133), which he knew were the only accounts that I really enjoyed working on. "Secondly, you as CEO tend to be a loose cannon, constantly throwing out new and often disruptive ideas for implementation. And I want to be sitting in your seat in ten years."

I gave him the buffing wheel accounts—and the chance to show off—that he asked for. I thanked him for telling me about my behavior and that I would try to be less disruptive in future, but I told him that he was unlikely to take my seat in ten years because another executive was ahead of him in service. "However," I said, "go out and find a company that suits us; we'll buy it; and you can be the CEO of the division." And he did just that.

After integrating the new company's operations with ours, I offered him the top position. To my complete surprise, he declined, explaining that the new company was mainly a sales organization and already had a young vice president who was its chief salesman. If he were not made president, he would lose his enthusiasm for the company. It was then that I knew he was our S.O.B. Shortly there-after, the executive who had been slated to lead the company died unexpectedly, and our young man was made president. The company grew like wildfire under his innovative leadership.

DON'T KILL MY MULE

he Jargon Society is a small press specializing in, although not limited to, poetry that was founded in 1951 by the poet Jonathan Williams when he was a student at Black Mountain College. I was president of the Society in 1983 when a young man, Ernest Mickler, brought us a book that he described as "a sort of *Uncle Remus* for white folks." He said he had shown it to almost every publisher of consequence. They all liked it but declined to consider publishing it unless he changed the title. This he refused to do because the title said it all: *White Trash Cooking*.

When I looked over the contents, which everyone at Jargon Press agreed were wonderful, I offered to put up most of the money for publication. The first edition almost instantly sold out. So we decided to try some advertising. (Among several publications we approached, *The New Yorker* responded that it would not print anything with such a title.) When Jargon Press started getting calls from other publishers wishing to buy the rights to the book, we decided to put it out for bids.

The third-highest—and successful—offer came from Ten Speed Press in Berkeley, California. Founder and publisher Phil Wood sent us a brilliantly conceived, very funny proposal that compared Ten Speed's office to our cookbook. It was creatively illustrated with photos from the book (like the *White Trash* ice box paired with snapshots of the Ten Speed office fridge). A photo of yard trash from the book was juxtaposed to stacks of manuscripts piled on Phil Wood's desk. And so on.

We signed the contract. By 2004, Ten Speed Press had sold over 800,000 copies of the book and published two sequels.

A FARMER HAD A MULE THAT WOULDN'T GEE OR HAW (TURN RIGHT OR LEFT) ON COMMAND. THE VETERINARIAN WAS SUMMONED AND HE PICKED UP A 2 X 4 PLANK AND HIT THE MULE ACROSS THE FOREHEAD.

■ ■ ■

"I WANTED YOU TO TRAIN MY MULE, NOT KILL HIM!" THE FARMER YELLED.

■ ■ ■

THE VET RESPONDED, "THAT'S RIGHT, BUT YOU HAVE TO GET HIS ATTENTION FIRST."

Sometimes, nay many times, the quality of a proposal will overcome a price differential. But it needs to be an attention grabber.

ROLL WITH THE PUNCHES
OR HOW WE PICKED UP A HOTEL

In 1979 I wanted to secure a grant from the Department of the Interior's Urban Development Action Grant (UDAG) division for the Stevens Center, an auditorium and performing arts center that was being planned for the North Carolina School of the Arts in Winston-Salem. The Stevens Center, named in honor of Roger Stevens (founding chairman of the National Endowment for the Arts and builder of the Kennedy Center), would also serve as home for the symphony, the opera, and other performing arts programs. At the time, UDAG was headed by Robert Embry, who was responsible for the redevelopment and revitalization of downtown Baltimore.

Research revealed that Embry would allow an applicant no more than 30 minutes for a presentation and would take any and all telephone calls that came in during that time. Because I am endowed with ADHD, constant interruptions don't work for me. Further research revealed that Embry's wife, Mary Ann Meers, was a sculptor whose work was displayed all over downtown Baltimore. I also knew that Embry had worked on the Baltimore project in concert with my friend Jim Rouse of the Rouse Company.

So I called Embry, and instead of setting up a regular meeting, I told him I was an art collector and would it be possible for me to get a car and a driver, visit with his wife in her studio, take her to lunch, and then let her guide me through downtown Baltimore while showing me her sculpture along the way. I then suggested that I take the Embrys to dinner, since my need to talk with him would take only about fifteen minutes and would hardly interrupt the flow of the occasion. He agreed to this.

At dinner I told Embry that I wanted $3 million for Winston-Salem from UDAG. Before I could get any further into my presentation, he raised his hand and he said that he was sorry to tell me that the whole UDAG bill was designated for the support of major cities such as New York, Chicago, Los Angeles, and Miami, and that a city of fewer than 3 or 4 million people would not qualify. I had missed this information in reading the bill. I said, "Bob, you just can't let me go home empty-handed."

He mentioned the name of a fellow who was trying to modify the UDAG bill with an amendment that would provide alot funds for the development of what were called "pockets of poverty." Embry gave me the man's phone number. When I returned home Sunday night, I called congressman Steve Neal, who told me that the UDAG bill was coming up for re-authorization on Wednesday, that he was on the committee, and that he would get in touch with the man in question. On Wednesday the amendment passed, and on Thursday, Winston-Salem's proposal was on Embry's desk.

We got our $3 million; but when I took the paperwork to Mayor Wayne Corpening, he put his arm around my shoulder and said, "Now, Phil, you know Winston-Salem needs a new hotel." I reminded him I had obtained that money specifically for the Stevens Center, but the mayor won the day.

Several months passed. I called the mayor who had managed to interest the Radisson Hotel people in the project, but there was a shortfall in the funding to pay for the construction. He had submitted a request to Alcoa Realty and had been turned down. I asked if I could step in, and he agreed.

I called Krome George, CEO of Alcoa, and said, "Krome, you, as chairman, put me on the Business Committee for the Arts (an organization established by David Rockefeller to persuade businesses to support the arts) and here I have an incredible opportunity to redevelop downtown Winston-Salem using the arts as a primary vehicle. But Alcoa Realty is turning down our request for a loan. I need you to call them up and tell them to give us the money." He did, and the city got its hotel. Working with Embry had required research, preparation, and imagination; working with Krome George was simply a matter of whom I knew. He was part of my network.

TWENTY YEARS' EXPERIENCE

"In this place it takes a lot of running to stay in the same place," said the Red Queen.

—LEWIS CARROLL, Through the Looking-Glass

An ensign on my destroyer, the USS *Zellars* DD777, gave an order to a chief petty officer, who questioned it on the grounds that he brought twenty years of experience to the table.

"No," the ensign responded. "You bring twenty years of the same experience versus twenty years of different experiences. Just because you have handled a situation this way before doesn't mean the same solution will work again in the same fashion."

In November of 2000, the Winston-Salem Alliance was formed to revitalize downtown Winston-Salem. All the local colleges and universities, as well as the major community organizations, were represented on the committee except for the North Carolina School of the Arts and the Winston-Salem Arts Council. I felt these omissions were a serious oversight because, as Jim Rouse (the most innovative American urban redeveloper of his day) once commented: "Shopping centers are convenience. Downtowns are arts and entertainment." Thus, it was clear to me that we needed representation from the arts and entertainment groups in our town. After I raised a big fuss, representatives from both organizations were added to the committee.

As I continued to think about it, however, I was concerned that the Alliance would be far too inclined to do things as they had been done in the past and that the large size of the committee would make decision-making cumbersome. I was reminded of a comment made in the late 1960s by Alvin Toffler, the author of *Future Shock:* "In the future, success would be achieved by hard-hitting ad-hocracies, and not by bureaucratic organizations."

The Alliance set about raising $47 million and hired a consultant who had worked on a revitalization project for Memphis, Tennessee. Then came the "recommendations," including a NASCAR bar and gallery, a $1.5 million Caribbean restaurant named for a famous basketball player with local connections, several bars and restaurants featuring Memphis-style jazz; and a $36 million restoration of an architecturally important office building that would be converted to 145 residential apartments. It was clear to me that all these projects would take years to achieve and any momentum would be lost before anything happened. Furthermore, I didn't think the "big box" approach would work.

Figuring there had to be a better way to achieve the same goals, I persuaded the mayor to appoint me Commissioner of Cultural Affairs. I hired an assistant, Chris Griffith, raised about $750,000 in loan funds for the Downtown Winston-Salem Partnership (DWSP), and started doing things our way.

In 1950 Meade Willis, a vice president of Wachovia Bank, had taken me on a tour of several rehabilitated urban neighborhoods. I was most impressed with New York City's Greenwich Village and SoHo districts. In 1963, I had spent four days in San Francisco's Haight-Ashbury. All three were once-rundown neighborhoods that had been energized and rejuvenated by a young and impecunious artistic community. This was the kind of vitality we were looking for.

So Chris and I sought out enterprising young people who were interested in the visual arts, the performing arts, and the culinary arts. Through them we heard that anyone trying to open a local gallery, performance venue, café, or small business would inevitably run into problems with local fire, health, and building inspectors. Today, to their credit, our city inspectors are more like coaches, helping merchants and other entrepreneurs navigate the maze of bureaucratic requirements and find the resources to accomplish their goals.

We soon persuaded the descendants of Meade Willis to establish a $500,000 low-interest loan fund for the DWSP to disburse to struggling urban pioneers with big dreams. Our city center is now bustling with shops, galleries, restaurants, cafés, and a street festival that draws 4,000 people weekly from May through early September—all thanks to loans from the city's special fund supplemented by the Willis Fund.

Chris and I felt very gratified when we read the *Winston-Salem Journal's* editorial on November 16, 2003: "What makes the development of downtown extra special is its local nature. The people who have opened businesses downtown are local. Sure, the city decision-makers talked to some development consultants and hired one to bring commercial and retail development to downtown. And maybe something will come of that effort someday. But if it doesn't, that's OK now. We're getting it done downtown locally."

These days the world is moving too swiftly for the bureaucratic leviathans of the past. This is the time for small, fast-moving adhocracies with strong leadership and the ability to make on-the-spot decisions. A committee can offer an opportunity for someone of vision and energy and ability to look like a leader, all the while checking his or her each and every move through consensus.

1. *Rules are established to create order and maintain profits for incumbents. Examples of rules are: social mores, professional licenses, government regulation, locked-up distribution channels.*

2. *Cheaper technology suddenly allows for the bypassing of rules.*

    —MICHAEL LEWIS, Next: The Future Just Happened

PART 3:
FUND-RAISING

"There's no use trying," said Alice. "One can't believe impossible things."

*"I dare say you haven't had much practice,"
said the Queen. "When I was your age I always did it
for half an hour a day. Why, sometimes I believed as
many as six impossible things before breakfast."*

—LEWIS CARROLL, Alice in Wonderland

here are literally hundreds of ways to raise money. One basic principle I have discovered after nearly a lifetime of fund-raising is that folks seldom give substantial sums to a nonprofit organization. People give to people—not to things or to organizations.

But, you say, I give annually to my church. Well, good for you, but think about this: Next time your annual subscription comes up for payment, think about how much you plan to contribute. Next, consider how much more you might give if another parishioner called on you in person for your contribution. Then think about how much more you might give if that visiting parishioner was a close friend and known to be a generous supporter of your church. In each case, as the contact becomes more and more personal, you will likely feel more and more of an obligation to give more and more money. People tend to give more when there is personal contact involved.

That said, it is important to develop your pitch so as to lead the prospect to consider larger goals. I use a basic outline for my pitches.

1. **Get your prospect's attention.** Clear the deck of extraneous matter—you don't allow your prospect multi-tasking here. Make a point of turning off your cell phone, signaling your prospect that this meeting is too important to take calls.

2. **Take note of your surroundings.** Look around the room.

Loads of freshly-cut flowers may indicate a love of gardening or an amateur horticulturalist. Lots of family photos? Ask about children and grandchildren. A model sailboat? A bowling trophy? Be sure to admire them and ask questions.

3. **Show interest in your prospect's interests.** Ask about recent local events in which she might have been involved. If you know she's a skier, ask where she has been or is planning to go skiing this season. If she's a traveler, ask about her recent past or upcoming future trips. The key is to focus the prospect on you and what you're saying.

4. **Now bring up the project.** Ask what your prospect knows about it. Then say that you wish to bring her up to date on it. Be as clear and concise as possible. This is not the moment for waffling.

5. **Ask for the donation.** This can be handled in a variety of ways. A) For a modest beginning, use "I have you down for $_____ amount." B) For a slightly more ambitious gift, try "Would you like to join me at $_____ dollar level?" C) For a more generous gift, place her in a category that's at least one level above her previous donation, "So, let's see, I have you down as a 'patron' this year." D) Finally, don't be afraid to shoot for the stars, "I'd like to see you in a leadership position regarding the project."

As I said earlier, there are literally hundreds of ways to raise money. Just as a sailor must in rough seas, be ready to alter your course. Because some folks get squirmy and uncomfortable when the topic of money (particularly theirs) comes up, find ways to break the tension. I have a store of amusing anecdotes, pithy sayings, jokes, and witticisms I like to use. Interesting illustrations or displays relevant to your project can be very useful at such moments.

Many people in business say they're no good at soliciting money. I say that learning how to solicit money is an invaluable skill for business. If I wanted to train a salesman, I'd hand him ten symphony tickets, tell him to sell them and come back with a report on each person who bought a ticket with an account of how he sold that ticket. If I wanted to train a banker in community relations, I'd suggest she form a committee to raise money for a hospital or a charity.

Fund-raisers for nonprofits can learn a lot from realtors and car dealers. How many times have you looked at a new car or house and the salesperson has said, "I know this is beyond your budget, but it's such a great car/ideal home, I can't resist showing it to you." The gauntlet has been subtly dropped. Many of us take the bait and spend more on a purchase than we ever intended. You, too, can throw down the gauntlet by showing your prospect the project's donors list. This list is usually divided into categories that start with Friend, proceed to Patron, followed by Sustainer, up to Benefactor. You might even highlight names of the prospect's friends who are listed in categories higher than that of her most recent gift. Above all, use your imagination. And if you sense resistance, be prepared to change course and use another technique.

THE WORLD'S BEST SALESMAN

Whatever you want to do in life has to start with you. No matter who you are or what you want to do, you must think of yourself as someone who can sell your ideas. If you look back over your life, whom would you identify as the greatest advocate of an idea, a concept, or a product? It can be anyone—parent, teacher, preacher—anyone. If you think you can sell to or influence others, you surely can think of someone who can sell to or influence you. Everybody can name someone. But the correct answer is that you are the best advocate for yourself; I am the best advocate for myself. Whether you are a salesperson, or a teacher or even a parent, you must think of yourself as someone who can sell your ideas. I often use the words salesperson and advocate; I could use several others, such as teacher or advertiser. Motivating your kids, making friends, or influencing other people require many of the same techniques. If I am the best salesman for myself, how can you persuade me to do what you wish?

Many years ago, several foundations organized a committee headed by John Filer, CEO of Aetna Life Insurance, to research charitable and philanthropic giving in the United States. The committee soon discovered that most large donors to a project, organization, or institution were also usually active participants in it. There was a direct correlation between the amount of time that donors volunteered and the amount of money those donors provided.

Persuade people to work in your nonprofit organization and they will tend to offer their financial support as well; when they become favorably and actively involved in it and enthusiastic about its goals, they tend to testify on its behalf. As religious institutions know, testimony yields support—and money. The best way to get someone committed to your project is testimony—which means he is selling himself. The United Way achieves this by asking volunteers to raise funds, which they do by speaking favorably about the United Way. Symphonies solicit testimony when they get volunteers to sell tickets. New organizations set up promotional advisory boards. There's always a way to get someone to testify. The person who testifies may not make a sale or successfully solicit money, but all the while he is selling himself.

There are lots of ways to set the hook. Your goal, remember, is to have the "mark" speak often and positively about your project. Getting someone to raise funds or sell tickets is the most effective short-term strategy. You cannot sell anything well without being in favor of it. A good long-term approach is to put people on a committee or a board and give them a specific assignment. Many religious and charitable groups use these techniques with obvious success.

When Nancy Hanks, chair of the National Endowment for the Arts, toured the United States to promote the NEA, she often encouraged her audiences to get involved by citing examples of successful arts programs. Her examples, however, were always located in large cities. Her intention was to show her audiences that it was not impossible to find money for the arts; unintentionally, she was implying "but you need to be in a major metropolis to do that." I suggested she ought also to include smaller cities and sent her information about the vibrant cultural life of my town.

Thereafter, she invariably used a Winston-Salem example in her presentations around the country. She was selling herself by constantly observing how successful Winston-Salem was and by pointing out that it was an average-sized city. It didn't hurt that her staff, who provided the preliminary approval of all NEA grants, were well aware that Winston-Salem was a favorite of hers—their boss, the chairman.

One technique I have employed regularly is the written testimonial. Think about inviting several people to send you something nice about your project to put in print. Most people will spend little time thinking about the assignment and their statements will not really address your concerns. If you ask several people, there will likely be some duplication of thought. To avoid useless statements or duplications, include, along with your request, a sample statement and say, "I'd appreciate it if you could write something along these

CHARLOTTE

My wife Charlotte began a tradition that we have sustained throughout our marriage. At various times, she has hidden greeting cards—some poking fun, others lamentably sentimental—in some most unusual places. I have found them on my pillow, at the dining table, in my car, or hidden in my suitcase when I travel. Inside each card she has added a thoughtful, handwritten message to me. When I started doing the same for Charlotte, I found myself giving a great deal of thought about my feelings for her as the perfect spouse, lover, and best friend. Over the years I have come to realize that this was, and still is, time well spent articulating my affection for her. I strongly recommend this kind of testimony to all couples. Flowers and gifts are important, but the time and effort required to select a suitable card and then write an additional heartfelt message will create a special kind of self-selling technique that can be a powerful bond after the nuptial knot has been tied.

lines." This will jump-start their thinking and make it much easier to find the words. Once they see their statements in print, they tend to become even more enthusiastic about the project.

I once sent actress Helen Hayes (whom I had enticed to join the Board of Visitors of the North Carolina School of the Arts) a suggested testimonial for the school's brochure. It was pretty flowery and she tore it up, writing, instead: "When anyone asks me where I can send my child for the best training in theater in America, I say, 'The North Carolina School of the Arts, none better!' " A year later she donated a fully endowed theater scholarship to the school.

FATHER KNOWS BEST

IF YOU WANT TO GO FROM ONE MOUNTAIN PEAK TO
ANOTHER, THE SHORTEST AND MOST DIRECT ROUTE CAN
OFTEN MEAN HAVING TO SCALE AN IMPOSSIBLY STEEP
CLIFF. TO GET TO YOUR GOAL THE BEST WAY, YOU OFTEN
HAVE TO FOLLOW THE LONGEST ROUTE. HIKERS CALL THIS
"ORIENTEERING."

■ ■ ■

In 1955 I completed a training course for budding executives at the Springs Cotton Mills; Colonel Elliott Springs let me
take the course as a favor to my father. I worked all three mills in the
small towns of Lancaster, Rock Hill, and Fort Mill, South Carolina,
and gained hands-on experience with every process—from opening
cotton bales to packaging finished bed sheets—and every piece of
equipment and machinery. I then went on to Hanes Dye and Finishing Company, doing every job but sweeping the floor, which was,
unfortunately, the job best suited to my talents.

Experience in New York City's garment district and our New York office followed. Then I hit the road, calling on Ford and General Motors in Detroit, the shoe businesses in Massachusetts, the buffing wheel trade in Chicago. On my return, I spent several months in the Winston office.

One morning, I stopped by my father's office and told him that I really did not want to spend the rest of my life dyeing pants pockets and waistbands, platform deckings or buffing wheel cloth. He asked what I did want to do.

"Winston-Salem has the first arts council in the United States," I said. "As a founding board member I have been consulting with cities across America. I see the arts council movement as being critical to the future development of the arts in this country and I feel I can have an important role in the movement."

"What role do you see an arts council playing?" he wanted to know.

"It would provide management for the arts community, and management is a scarce commodity in the arts."

"What's the most important job a council can do?"

"Fund-raising assistance," I responded.

My father rose from his chair, told me to stay there, and left the room, closing the door behind him. When he returned he was dressed as though for an important meeting—tie straight, hair freshly combed, and jacket neatly buttoned. He said, "Mr. President of the Company, I am Phil Hanes, Executive Director of the Winston-Salem Arts Council. We are having our capital fund drive and want your company to give $10,000."

Then he left the room. When he returned he was in shirt sleeves, with tie at half-mast and hair slightly mussed. "Howdy, my friend," he said. "I haven't seen you since we worked together on the United Fund drive. A real success and you played an important part in it. There's this organization that's relatively new in town called the Arts Council and, speaking as one corporate exec to another, I think we should help out. I'd like to put you down for $10,000."

Once again my father kept me sitting there a few minutes while he left the room. When he came back he asked, "Who do you think got the money?"

Reluctantly I said, "The second one."

"Son," he said, "there are two ways to go through life if you have a goal such as yours. One is to take the job you think you would most enjoy, and do the best you can. The other is to focus on what you wish to accomplish and take the logical path to get there. I suggest that you do a good job here and one day sit in this chair as a successful businessman with a good record of community participation and then you can accomplish most of your goals. The road to success is not always a direct one."

I took his advice and he was right.

HE LEADETH ME
INTO GREEN PASTURES

When, in my continuous quest to sell someone on one of my local projects, I am expecting a visit from, say, the representative of a foundation or a journalist who will provide me with publicity, I attempt to encourage a longer visit than is actually required to promote the project. This is because I want to show my visitor some of the environment surrounding the project. As we start our tour, I say, "You know, you might want to live here someday."

Suppose you live in New York and you've gone through a hard winter. Or maybe you are reaching retirement age. In any case, you might just have a lingering thought of moving to a smaller, more manageable city with a more benign climate. What does an extended visit to my city achieve? It adds a whole new dimension to your visit, and makes you far more attentive to my project. In the back of your mind is a small voice saying, "I might like to live here."

Bennett Schiff was for years the arts editor of the *Smithsonian* magazine. He was such a delightful man that Winston-Salem had little trouble showing him its best face. He ran three articles in his magazine, including a cover story on the North Carolina School of the Arts. He did not, in fact, move to our city, but for years he and his wife returned often to visit.

When trying this ploy, do at least a modicum of research. If your visitor cannot eat shellfish, best not go to a seafood restaurant. If there's a choice between going to a dance performance or an opera, consider her personal preferences. And, if it is at all possible, arrange that she visit a home or two in the community, where she is treated as friend and not just as an impersonal benefactor. She'll be more likely to appreciate the green pastures.

FORCE FIT

A little research into the interests of a benefactor is never a waste of time and can, on occasion, yield funds from unlikely sources. When raising money, many organizations, for obvious reasons, apply only to those funding sources that give to their specialty. Nonetheless, I once raised $200,000 for the North Carolina School of the Arts from a foundation that was (and still is) interested primarily in the delivery of health care.

Wake Forest University's Baptist Hospital provides health care to small communities in the mountains of northwest North Carolina, and the Steele Reece Foundation of New York City, with a view to funding the program, sent its representative to investigate. During the morning of his visit, I took the representative to meet with the doctors involved. Over lunch I found out that he played drums when he was in the military. I made a quick call to the North Carolina School of the Arts and set up the following scenario. I told our visitor that we had some free time that afternoon and we would visit the School of the Arts in Winston-Salem.

During our tour of the school, there "happened" to be a percussion class in session. I asked the teacher, Massey Johnson, if we could come in, explaining that our distinguished visitor had played the drums in the Army. Massey asked my guest for a demonstration. Naturally, everyone was enthralled, and our visitor stayed for the class.

Afterward, I told him it was my experience that small mountain towns had very little trouble in attracting doctors or teachers who enjoyed deer hunting and trout fishing and the like, but what was there for their spouses to do? Doctors and schoolteachers are busy and productive, but their spouses, too, have strong intellects and varied interests. It is difficult to find stimulation for such interests in small rural towns.

The North Carolina School of the Arts was eager for its senior students and faculty to perform around the state, but it takes time and organization to arrange such tours. I told him about the town of Sparta, which usually produced a couple of professional perform-ances each year. I suggested that the North Carolina School of the Arts could provide such performances at a much lower cost than the professional groups coming in from New York City would charge and the quality would be as good, perhaps better, in some cases. The same amount of money the small town was spending on two per-formances annually could easily pay for four. This would require a small board that would occupy the spouses' interest and perhaps keep the doctor and teacher in the small town.

Then I asked if the Steele Reece Foundation would like to offer a 50-percent matching grant fund as a five-year experiment. We put in the application and were given $200,000 to support the project. The money was disbursed over a five-year period to small Appalachian towns so that they could hire performing artists from the North Carolina School of the Arts. What was, on the surface, a forced fit turned out to be a fine fit.

BANKER'S CH♀ICE

Organizations live and die by their boards. The successful ones have members from all walks of life, individuals with the range of skills that the organization needs to stay afloat. The Chamber of Commerce and the United Way, for instance, have little trouble getting key executives of a bank to sit on their boards—and to provide financial expertise. Arts organizations, at least in the South, are not so fortunate. The Winston-Salem Symphony wanted to build a stronger board, and a couple of us who were already on the board went to a local bank and suggested to the president that we would like a young executive, a potential future officer of the bank, to be the co-chair of the symphony's annual fund-raising campaign. Duties would include building a strong organization and selling a product that was not easy to sell.

We suggested to the president that he identify his top three up-and-coming executives, and we selected a young man whom we thought likely to be a good fit. "Your boss at the bank has his eye on you," we told him. "Here's your opportunity to really show him what you can do. If you do a good job, your chances for promotion should be excellent. We're confident you'll do the best job, but this is a tough challenge. If you have any hesitancy about undertaking it, your boss gave us a couple of other names."

We also explained we were assigning to him a mentor, a co-chairman who was familiar with the idiosyncratic nature of the symphony, its members, and its activities. When the young banker accepted the job, we put him on the board and gave him a list of the major potential donors. Throughout the fund-raising campaign, we saw to it that his name appeared constantly in the press and that, each time, he was associated with the bank. Eventually, we went to his boss and we said, "Look what a great job your protégé is doing." We produced the press clippings, carefully highlighting the young exec's name along with the name of the bank.

It is generally true that during a fund-raising campaign, 80 percent of the donated dollars come from 20 percent of the donors. We told the bank president that his employee had done very well with certain people in the 20-percent category, but that he had failed with four or five calls. Then we asked the president how we could help his employee get money from clients who seemed to be holding out.

Recall, when we chose the young executive from the short-list of three, we were supporting the president's first choice. Then we gave him the opportunity to do something that would also reflect well on the bank, thus confirming the rightness of the president's choice. Suddenly, he had a fair shot at becoming his boss's successor.

Furthermore, because of the young man's visibility in our campaign, the reputation of the bank was somewhat at stake. At this point we had very little trouble getting the president to take the critical leadership position in our fund-raising effort, which we had needed from the beginning. Now the president felt that funding for the symphony was about his man and his bank, and he had a vested interest to see both succeed. Therefore, he found it no trouble to call reluctant donors and add an extra pitch or arrange for a better approach at a much higher level.

This strategy would have long-range benefits as well. After the campaign ended, invariably the young executive would move up, and there would be constant reminders that his work on behalf of the symphony had been very helpful to his career. As he rose through the ranks, he would associate his success with the symphony, and in the future he would see to it that the symphony did well by the bank. Perhaps he had always been interested in music; now his interest had vested.

THE VESTED-INTEREST PLOY

TWO MEN WERE WALKING DOWN THE STREET WHEN THEY
NOTICED A MAN OBVIOUSLY AVOIDING THEM BY CROSSING
THE STREET AND THEN CROSSING BACK AGAIN. ONE MAN
SAID TO THE OTHER, "WHY DID HE AVOID US?"

"DAMNED IF I KNOW," CAME THE REPLY. "I NEVER DID A
FAVOR FOR HIM IN MY LIFE."

■ ■ ■

When you play chess, you rely on smart ploys—carefully worked out strategies designed to get you where you want to go. When my goal is to get someone to do something, there are two ploys that I use constantly. In fact, they often overlap each other. I will ask someone, "Suppose you have a very close relative in serious trouble and I am the only one who can resolve the problem. On request, I do so at considerable effort. Who is indebted to whom?" The response is invariably, "I am indebted to you." Most people do not wish to feel obligation—and usually try to return the favor to "get out of debt."

But it is the vested interest that turns inclination into commitment and, thus, it is the vested interest that must be cultivated. Think of the individual or organization to which you have donated more than any other. If that person or organization needed even more assistance, wouldn't you seriously consider it? In times of financial distress, the best sources of additional funding will often be those who have already given more than their share. The fact is, the more vested the interest a person holds in another person or project, the more he is prepared to give. That is why it is so important to receive favors of time and/or money and never repay them. Learn to become indebted, but don't forget to show your continuing appreciation, which is the second ploy. Appreciation comes in many guises: thank-you notes, news stories, mentions in programs or annual reports, awards—all are grateful acknowledgments of indebtedness.

The retail merchants in our city didn't, for whatever reason, seem to have much of an interest in classical music or our local symphony orchestra. I was asked to see if I couldn't change that. So I went to see Willie Belle Dixon, the manager of Montaldo's, a high-end women's clothing boutique in Winston-Salem. Before my visit with Willie Belle, I used a technique derived from yoga: In order to relax make yourself as taut as possible; then relax, and then you tighten up again. When you subsequently let go, you are relaxed.

I knew that Montaldo's, like most other retailers in town, pur-chased a certain amount of advertising annually from the newspaper, so the ad space was already paid for. I also knew how challenging it could be to produce new ads, day in and day out, with a continually fresh approach.

"Willie Belle," I said, "I want to ask you for a big favor." (I could see her tense up here.) "If I were to ask you to help with the chamber of commerce or the United Way, your response would be, 'How much?' not 'How come?' But if I said to you, 'It's for the arts and, in this case, the symphony,' you would probably question whether you wanted to assist at all. So this is difficult because the symphony needs your help.

"Here's what I'm looking for. On opening night, October 5, I want to try to dress up the house in black tie. Would you consider taking out a full-page ad showing a woman in one of your evening gowns stepping out of a fancy car in front of Reynolds Auditorium? The caption would read something like, 'For the opening of the Winston-Salem Symphony season, buy your frock at Montaldo's.' "

Willie Belle had little interest in the symphony, but when she heard my idea, she relaxed. She was glad to do it because there was something in it for her. After the concert Willie Belle received dozens of letters from her most loyal clients (all carefully scripted by the manager of the symphony) praising her for contributing to the success of the evening. Each letter stressed how much the writer, as a symphony patron or board member, was indebted to Montaldo's and to Willie Belle Dixon for so elegantly dressing up the house. Montaldo's was also listed in the program as a symphony donor and supporter.

About a month later Willie Belle, who now had a vested interest in the symphony's success, made a nice donation. Using Montaldo's as a bellwether, we were able to get additional support from other retailers in town.

THE HONEY DO GAMBIT

In 2003, I attended my first meeting of the board of the H. John Heinz III Center for Science, Economics, and the Environment. The chairman was G. William Miller, who has held several major corporate posts and was a former Secretary of the Treasury. Other board members included prominent business people, scientists, economists, and other experts. The Heinz Center produces top-notch unbiased reporting on the world's ecosystems, and its publications, while geared toward those who advocate for the maintenance of a livable planet, receive widespread international attention.

One of the organization's primary concerns is getting this information to national and international opinion-makers, decision-makers, and leaders—a clear and straightforward goal. And it is vital for those of you within an organization to be clear on what you want to achieve. But, if you want others to participate, you need to make it worth their while. This is the vested-interest ploy.

An organization such as the Heinz Center—whose product is information—could be expected to have, among its various committees (finance, nominations, development, and executive) a public relations committee. The Heinz Center did not. Their development committee planned to ask a select group of corporate CEOs to join an advisory committee and pledge an annual contribution of $50,000 as an indication of their companies' interest in world ecology. It was suspected there might be few takers.

Those suspicions were not groundless: almost as few people, I suggested, would want to join a so-called second-tier advisory committee as would wish to be members of a development committee. Titles are important. So, a decision was made to name the group the Heinz Center Business Council for Science and the Environment. All agreed that it should be possible to get the money, but how would the CEOs be induced to listen to the same message and participate in the same discussion year after year?

I suggested it might be possible if their annual event—an update on the health of U.S. ecosystems—were designed to be of interest also to the spouses. Corporate executives routinely attend such events, while their spouses either stay home or find themselves at the event but left to their own devices. An exciting entertainment package for all attendees, with special events scheduled during meeting times, would encourage spouses to participate; their interest would be vested also. This technique is known as the "Honey Do" gambit, as in, "Honey, I really do want to go to this event."

Additionally, I suggested we invite members of the Young Presidents Organization, who would be asked to contribute a lesser sum, say, $25,000. The YPOs would appreciate being invited to participate in such high-level meetings with more experienced executives, and those execs would enjoy getting to know the young up-and-comers whom they might wish to hire for their own companies, or whose companies they might wish to buy. Then I suggested the Heinz Center staff make a list of private foundation board members from which Heinz might expect to receive money for this venture and choose some of its Council members from that list, thus getting prominent people for its Council as well as access to the foundation—two for one.

Here's a case in which you not only wish to raise money ($1 million for this one), but also you want key people to attend the meeting and get the message. The strategy uses the spouse to put the needed body in the chair.

RAISING MONEY

The influence of real art can be seen in my (furniture)
titles and in my emphasis on textures and humor as
expressive mediums. I directly ally artists' techniques to
my furniture all of the time because I like going to parties
with real artists.

—GARRY KNOX BENNETT, Made in Oakland

In 1962, Terry Sanford, the governor of North Carolina, approached McNeil Lowry of the Ford Foundation with a request for a large grant to fund a new school of the performing arts. Mr. Lowry asked, "What will happen if we don't support this idea?"

"Then," the governor replied, "we won't ask you to the party." He got the money.

Guests always have obligations and folks who are miserly don't get invited to the party. When they know they have to pay for the privilege, they can often be persuaded if their names appear on a list of event sponsors, especially if the list includes many of their most respected peers. The sponsors' list is a useful tool: it encourages people to pay to go to the party, and it acknowledges the generosity of those who do.

I remember when I persuaded a local arts organization to list its sponsors by donation categories, such as Patron, Sponsor, and Benefactor, depending on the size of the donation. The list was published over the strong objection of the president who, it was revealed, had been donating only a pittance. Although he could have chosen to resign, instead, to his credit, he sprang for the top category, understanding that you have to join the club to come to the banquet.

Raising money from individuals takes homework if you want to understand what motivates them, but there are some generalizations that apply universally:

1. **Wealthy people are often wealthy because they are miserly, hoarding their cash and spending much of their time watching the Dow and the S&P.**

I go regularly to an exclusive spa in California. The television set in the spa's only sitting room is always tuned to the stock market. Copies of the *Wall Street Journal* are carried around like Bibles by the spa's guests. Some of these guys are extremely civic-minded, but their depth of knowledge regarding the needs of ordinary people is questionable. So, when raising a subject unfamiliar to them, you will find it useful to approach it slowly, so that your information does not outstrip their understanding. If it's not a market-based idea, refurbish it in terms they can understand.

Several years ago, I was asked to address the members of a country club in Birmingham, Alabama, about the benefits of an art center located in the central business district as a tool for downtown redevelopment. Before my speech, Winton "Red" Blount (one of the members and the man who, at an arts symposium I once attended at a YPO conference in the Bahamas, had asked when I was going to stop playing with "all those fairies") cautioned me: "Phil, you better be careful what you say here. You know that Birmingham considers itself the red-neck capital of the world."

Now, it is widely known that it is easy to tell a red neck, but you can't tell him much. Most of the people in my audience were sitting stiffly in their chairs, drinks in hand. I had to engage them, so I began: "I want to point out to you the importance of the arts in your downtown." (I could see the backs stiffen.) "I've been told I might be on thin ice here since Birmingham considers itself to be the red-neck capital of the world. This reminds me of some traveling actors whose director approached the proprietor of an inexpensive boarding house in Biloxi, Mississippi. 'Madam, do you have terms for strolling thespians?' 'Yes,' she said. 'Bastard and son of a bitch.' "

My audience laughed. Then I told them that I wanted to touch them on the spondulik nerve, "the nerve that connects the heart to

91

the pocket book." By now I had their attention and could relate the experiences of other cities whose downtown districts had clearly benefited when an arts center had been developed. And, among oher examples, I could point to the work of Jim Rouse, the developer who had successfully rebuilt urban areas of Baltimore, Norfolk, New York, and Philadelphia. I also reminded them that artists continue to revitalize the boroughs of Manhattan, moving from Greenwich Village, to SoHo, to NoHo, to TriBeCa, to Chelsea, and Williamsburg.

As for Winton Blount, years later he "got religion" and hired a curator who helped him and his corporation to acquire a major art collection. He then founded Alabama's renowned Shakespeare Theater and spoke on the vital role of the arts all over the United States. I find that as people get enough money and power to suit their fancies, they often turn to the arts. Curious . . .

2. **Most folks think that because a person has money, he's a good target. Chances here are probably no better than fifty-fifty.**

When I was on the board of Charleston's Spoleto Festival, I was told by an extremely wealthy man that he and his wife had missed only one festival since its beginnings. Such enthusiasm was worth tapping into, so I persuaded his wife to join the board. About a year later, I dropped them a note in which I said that the minimum annual donation of $5,000 was fine for those with limited resources, but those of us who could do more were supposed to step a bit closer to the plate. He responded that he considered my letter inappropriate and she resigned forthwith.

3. **The children and grandchildren of founders of large foundations tend to believe that the buck has already stopped before they ever arrived on the scene.**

Because their forebears created a charitable resource with funds they otherwise might have inherited, they themselves feel under no obligation to share. It is a waste of time and energy to look to them personally for further support; they are likely to be helpful only as sources for recommendations to their family foundations.

4. **People with hobby-horses tend not to travel far.**

In the eighteenth-century novel *The Life and Opinions of Tristram Shandy*, Uncle Toby always rode his hobby-horse. And so it is with many people of means. More than once, in an attempt to get someone to support community projects other than her own hobby-horse, my cousin Gordon and I have offered a quid pro quo: "You give to this organization and we'll match it with a gift to yours." Perhaps surprisingly, this in itself was a hard sell; and it never shook loose additional money for other projects, even when these were in the same field and beneficial to the hobby-horse rider's own organization.

A variant is the important community or college facility bearing

93

the family name. This is their Trojan Hobby-Horse, the defense weapon of choice, wherein reside the supposed continuing benefactions of the heirs. When asked for additional assistance, the hypothetical Mr. J. B. Glotz gives that knowing glance at the edifice on the hill named for the Glotzes. One immediately understands that the possibility of additional donations is not to be entertained.

The American Association of Fund Raising Councils (AAFRC) annually publishes information about where philanthropic money goes. In 2002, $84 billion went to religious institutions. To some of these donors, regular contributions to a church, synagogue, temple, mosque, etc., may serve to replace or substitute for other kinds of active community support and/or involvement.

I like to invoke the words of the poet Kenneth Patchen, from his book entitled *Fables:* "A good day's work never hurt anyone. This is particularly true of those who make a habit of preaching this." Often, those who are most vociferous in board meetings are often the least generous donors or doers.

It is a well-established fact that most of any fund-raising campaign's money will come from a tiny percentage of its donors, those rare birds called "generous givers." To my mind, these are the true children of God.

5. Names are very important.

The aforementioned Trojan Hobby-Horse notwithstanding, one

way to raise money is to find something you can name for the individual. Failing that, there is always the name in the annual report. This acknowledgment is meaningful to most donors, and some will attach unusual importance to this.

Many, many years ago, when I was on the board of the Winterthur Museum in Delaware, the Internal Revenue Service advised us that, because most of the museum's funding came from the du Pont family itself, the museum would be required to account for its finances under a particular tax-exempt category, one that is applicable to a hobby organization. This requirement would cost the foundation a huge amount of money in taxes. The IRS granted Winterthur a reasonable period of time to increase the percentage of its funds donated by outsiders. There was considerable wringing of hands because the board members had never had to pursue consequential funds beyond its own resources.

I suggested that, as I was a board member of the Old Salem restoration in Winston-Salem, I could persuade a sizable number of our most loyal contributors to make their gifts to Winterthur in exchange for equal funding from the most loyal Winterthur donors. To me this seemed so elegantly simple: the same amount of money in donations and considerably less money paid out in taxes.

"Oh, absolutely not!" was the response. "We don't want our names elsewhere. We want our names on Winterthur!" Even at the cost of many thousands of dollars.

This kind of thinking was firmly entrenched. When the founder of Winterthur died, the chef who had served him and who had catered many events for the du Pont family was moved from his former employer's home to the reception center restaurant. But the lunch and dinner traffic in the restaurant was insufficient to support his salary. The question was: How to get more lunchtime trade?

I pointed out that there were numerous museums around Wilmington, all of them supported by different du Ponts, although the circuitous roads made it difficult to find them. This could be solved if Winterthur published a map with some suggested itineraries that would make lunch at the reception center the obvious choice.

Again, the response was indignation: "Why in the world would we want to publicize those other museums?" Eventually, the chef had to move away.

6. Names are very important even in the hereafter.

There is always The Bequest. One approaches the target with the downcast eyes of the undertaker, Digger O'Dell, and in reverential tones refers to the potential demise of one who might wish his persona remembered by future generations. This is an important source of funds. In 2002, it represented 7.5 percent of donated dollars in the U.S., compared with 11.2 percent from foundations and 5.1 percent from corporations. People do like to feel that they have left some form of golden spoor.

I like to spread around the tale of the Pig in the Barnyard, in hopes of a change in attitude.

■ ■ ■

THE PIG ASKED THE CHICKEN, "WHAT MAKES YOU SO POPULAR?"

THE CHICKEN SAID, "I GIVE MY EGGS."

TO THIS SAME QUESTION, THE HORSE RESPONDED, "I PULL THE PLOW AND GIVE RIDES." THE COW SAID SHE GAVE MILK, AND THE DOG SAID HE GAVE PROTECTION.

"WELL," SAID THE PIG INDIGNANTLY, "I GIVE MY ALL— MY BACON, HAM, CHOPS, EVERYTHING!! WHY AM I NOT AS POPULAR AS YOU?"

"YOU WAIT UNTIL YOU'RE DEAD TO DO IT!"

■ ■ ■

STOP TOOTING YOUR HORN

OUR LONDON TAXI STALLED AND STOPPED JUST AS THE
LIGHT CHANGED FROM RED TO GREEN. AN ANGRY LADY
BEHIND US STARTED BLOWING HER HORN. AFTER A FEW
BLASTS, OUR DRIVER WENT OVER TO HER AND SAID,
"LADY, IF YOU WILL COME START MY TAXI, I'LL SIT ON YOUR
HORN TILL IT STARTS."

∎ ∎ ∎

I can't write this book without referring to the adage, "Try
to accomplish the possible and leave the impossible alone." In fund-
raising circles, you'll often hear the suggestion, "Go to Mr. X for
money. He's rich, spends tons of money on palatial houses, hunts
and fishes in far-away lands, and takes exotic trips in his private
plane." When someone in the community tells you Mr. X is, in fact,
a parsimonious donor even to those organizations on whose boards
he sits, I would advise you not to waste your time and energy. Self-
indulgence seldom produces beneficence of real consequence.

There are some folks who can be moved, but require an inordinate amount of effort to push them an inch. And sometimes you have to find this out the hard way. I once spent three years courting a Mrs. M. and did her a great number of favors, all in the hope that she would loosen her purse strings. I had been told that her donations went only to her pet causes or to the few organizations that bolstered her feelings of self-importance. But I was sure she liked me and would repay me for some of those favors. I was wrong. I could have spent my time and energy far more profitably elsewhere. There is no point in beating your head against a wall, and it saves much aggravation and time if you pick your targets among the doers rather than try to convert the showy hobby-horse cowboys.

It's nearly always true: if you want to get a job done, ask a busy person to help you do it. Someone who has lots of resources and lots of time can actually impede your progress. The reason he has lots of time on his hands is precisely because he doesn't really engage.

On a trip through the English countryside, our taxi reached a yield area where the lady in the car ahead of us seemed reluctant to pull over into the vacant spaces between other cars. Our driver approached her and said, "Lady, that sign says GIVE WAY—not GIVE UP." His efforts to move her met with success. So may it happen unto you.

THE AMEN CORNER

I have visited almost every island in the Caribbean that does not have a golf course. One of the real attractions for me is Sunday service in an island church (often Moravian). There is always local color, wonderful music, and splendid singing that's fairly bursting with spontaneous joy and enthusiasm. And worshipers in the "amen corner" punctuate the pertinent points throughout the service with cries of "Praise the Lord," "That's right," or "Amen, Brother!" I can't think about the Caribbean without remembering fondly this obvious delight in the Lord's message.

In 1968, Gordon Braithwaite, who was an NEA staff member of Jamaican descent, called to tell me that Hernan Padilla, the incoming mayor of San Juan, Puerto Rico, had run for election on an arts platform, assuring voters that the arts would bring new vibrancy to old San Juan. He had asked Gordon to send someone to the island in September to help raise $200,000 in private funds to accomplish this. Gordon tapped me to go. I said I had never been to Puerto Rico and added, "Besides, it's too damn hot there in September." Gordon reminded me that he had helped me get some funding for Winston-Salem and now he wanted to cash in a chip. So I agreed.

Some research of corporations with major operations in Puerto Rico turned up my cousin's company, Hanes Hosiery, and Union Carbide, where I had a good friend. A couple of phone calls secured their pledges of $10,000 apiece—and the beginnings of an amen corner. Gordon and I flew down to meet with Mayor Padilla. Gordon must have given him a whole passel of trash talk because I was treated like visiting royalty, put up in a great hotel in the old city, well fed, and lavishly entertained. He even persuaded the delightful philanthropist and former governor, Louis Ferre, to take me to Ponce to see the art museum that housed Ferre's fabulous collection of old master paintings.

I asked the mayor to arrange a breakfast for the leaders of local companies who might go along with a $10,000 pledge, in addition to the two companies I had already committed. He brought six people to the meal. Using the domino gambit, I made my pitch and said I already had commitments from Hanes Hosiery and Union Carbide. All six agreed to pledge.

The next night representatives from the eight companies were joined by a large number of other corporate officers and their spouses at a lavish cocktail party given by one of the mayor's major supporters in his gorgeous home. After the appropriate liquid lubrication, the host made several flattering remarks about Mayor Padilla, who then spoke about his program to boost San Juan through the arts. I then described the success of the arts as an urban development tool and asked if the major corporations doing business on the island would each pledge $10,000. When I asked for responses, I glanced over to my amen corner—and, as if on cue, my allies responded one after another. Picking up on their enthusiasm, the others followed and we raised the funds. Hernan Padilla sent me a lovely certificate in appreciation, and I thanked him for a nonpareil experience. What a lovely and hospitable city!

PART 4

PROBLEM-SOLVING

> *Ask stupid questions.*
> *Growth is fueled by desire and innocence.*
> *Assess the answer. Not the question.*
> *Imagine learning through your life at the rate of an infant.*
>
> —BRUCE MAU, "An Incomplete Manifesto
> for Growth"

So you're faced with a challenge. Start solving it by giving it a positive name: call it an opportunity. Next, make it as simple as you can by breaking it into small pieces. Arrange the pieces in the order you wish to address them and then address them one at a time.

Often it helps to look at the situation in different ways:

- Can you turn it upside down or inside out?

- Can you diminish or enlarge it?

- Could the sequence of its parts be reversed or reordered?

- Can you brainstorm about the situation with others?

Embroidered on a pillow on the couch in my office is the title of a speech I once heard: "Anything worth doing is worth doing poorly." If you have a dilemma or a challenge to work with, don't wait around until boredom sets in and you put it aside or someone else takes away and runs with it. GET MOVING! No matter what, take that first step. And correct mistakes as you go along. If you had the whole solution before you started, you wouldn't have the problem in the first place. A few setbacks along the way are insignificant compared to the total failure of not solving the problem itself.

The Japanese have a useful technique called *kaizen*—take one small step at a time, but keep moving forward. When obstacles appear, meet them head on or go over, under, or around them. There is usually a way.

Several year ago, a warehouse belonging to one of the largest manufacturers of blue jeans in the United States flooded, causing considerable damage to the color of the denim. Transforming disaster into opportunity, the manufacturer advertised their new item as "distressed denims." And they're still selling, although today the company has figured out how to replicate the mottled appearance without flooding their warehouses.

Look for what's good about your problem.

Many years ago I read an article in *Reader's Digest* about the history of American advertising. Included was an account of two salmon fishermen who built a cannery in Alaska so that they could earn a living while pursuing their favorite sport. But the local salmon species had white flesh, and the fishermen were having a tough time marketing it. Instead of giving up, they dealt with the problem head on and promoted their brand as "salmon that won't turn pink in the can." Of course, today such a claim would be illegal. Too bad! Folks today just can't take a joke.

Try to make lemonade out of a lemon.

In 1978, when Winston-Salem's Contributions Council (which sets the calendar for major civic fund-raising projects) rejected the bid of the North Carolina School of the Arts to raise $6 million for a performing arts center, I went to Washington D.C. and collected a little more than half that sum in federal grants, then got permission to complete the funding locally.

Find another route to your goal.

When various members of the Wilson family turned aside my efforts to purchase the 9,000-acre side of Mount Mitchell I went back year after year after year for twelve years, until I persuaded them to sell it to our trout fishing club.

Persistence!

In short, if you believe you have a good idea, go for it, don't wait, move! Jump in as though it was meant to be, and then stick with it in spite of the obstacles. Certain projects that begin on an impulse may take years to complete.

■ THE MOST EFFICIENT COMMITTEES CONSIST OF THREE ■
PEOPLE, TWO OF WHOM ARE ABSENT.

For fifty years, I joined one committee after another, the aim of each being the attempted revitalization of downtown Winston-Salem. All my suggestions were ignored, so in 2000 I decided to go it alone and hired my able partner Chris Griffith. In a little over two and a half years, we have supported a bevy of new restaurants, cafés, bars, art galleries and performance spaces—sidewalk dining and a vibrant arts district—the perfect confluence of art and commerce. And we did it with only the assistance of money loaned at low interest to enterprises that no bank would even consider. Much of what we accomplished was based on my four-day experience in San Francisco's Haight-Ashbury district in 1968. This model demonstrated to me that it is young people—with dreams and determination and guts— that will renew a city. The old folks in expensive suits who head for the suburbs in expensive cars at 5 P.M. will not.

Believe in your intuition.

SELL 'EM WHAT THEY WANT, EVEN IF THEY DON'T KNOW THEY WANT IT

It stands to reason that creative people engaged in creative projects will benefit from creative management. In fact, people engaged in managing arts organizations, and the artists they showcase, are sometimes highly creative themselves. Among the most creative was Ralph Black, who managed the National Symphony Orchestra in the 1950s.

Mrs. Jouett Shouse chaired the board at that time and later donated her beautiful estate, Wolf Trap, as a performing arts center. For years she vied annually with Mrs. Marjorie Merriweather Post, who chaired the National Opera Board, to see who could give the best party. One year Mrs. Shouse planned her party around a concert to be given by the pianist Oscar Levant.

On the day of the performance, Ralph Black went to the station in Washington D.C. to meet Levant's train. The pianist's manager approached Ralph on the platform and said that he was very sorry, but the maestro was not feeling well and would be traveling on to Atlanta.

"He can't do this to us!" Ralph gasped.

The manager replied, "Well, you can try to talk him out of it."

Ralph found Oscar Levant hunkered down in bed, his head wrapped in a towel.

"Maestro," said Ralph, "we're all so distressed to hear of your indisposition. Naturally, we wouldn't want you to play here in the nation's capital when you're feeling less than your best. Especially since key members of the House and Senate will be coming, along with several ambassadors and even some cabinet members. We are hopeful the president might come. It's been touted as the biggest concert of the year. But, if you're not feeling up to snuff, we certainly understand.

"Fortunately, we have an excellent substitute. He is by no means your equal, but he is a real 'comer,' a young pianist who has a brilliant career ahead of him. This concert may prove to be his big opportunity.

"So, please don't worry about a thing, Maestro. My only concern is the orchestra. The musicians have looked forward all year to this performance with you. I'm sure they'll all understand why you won't play when you're not at your best, but perhaps you can do them a small favor. Do you think you could just run through the rehearsal with them? It would give them such a thrill! If you feel up to doing that, I can get you on the late afternoon train to Atlanta immediately afterward."

Levant agreed. Ralph rushed back to his office and called several congressmen, inviting them to the rehearsal. As each one arrived at the symphony hall, he was given a slip of paper on which Ralph had written a suggestion about what to say when meeting Levant after the rehearsal.

As agreed, Levant rehearsed with the orchestra. When he returned to his dressing room, he was greeted by several of Washington's political elite. Each was effusively enthusiastic. Thanks to the script provided beforehand, the comments about the rehearsal indicated a considerable knowledge of music.

Following the improvised meet-and-greet, Oscar Levant turned to Ralph Black and said: "I feel much better. I think I would like to play tonight after all."

During the performance later that evening, Ralph was sitting backstage in the dressing room with Levant's manager.

"You know," said Ralph, "if Oscar Levant doesn't show up for Mrs. Shouse's party tonight after this performance, my head will roll!"

"Party?" asked the manager. "Levant never goes to parties."

"Oh . . . god," said Ralph. "Get out of here and let me talk with him." After a long series of curtain calls, Oscar Levant returned to his dressing room to find Ralph sitting slouched in a chair—shoes off, tie undone, shirt open at the top.

"Wow, what a concert!" Ralph gushed. "You played magnificently. I'm completely overwhelmed and exhausted. Thank God I don't have to do anything now except meet a couple of friends for dinner at a little bistro with really good food and wine, and we can relive this wonderful evening."

Levant asked if he could join them. Once in the car, Ralph drove circuitously through downtown Washington and into a residential area. Then, before Levant knew what was happening, they pulled up in front of Mrs. Shouse's house. As Ralph opened the car door, Levant was greeted effusively by Mrs. Shouse with the raucous sounds of a full-blown party wafting from behind her front door.

Levant muttered under his breath, "Black, you bastard!" But he stayed. The next morning, Ralph escorted a red-eyed Levant to his train.

"Black!"

"Yes, Maestro?"

"Black, I want you to do me a favor. Call the manager of the Atlanta Symphony. Tell him I'm indisposed and I'm going on to Miami."

NAPOLEON'S TOMB

Napoleon's Tomb in Paris is a magnificent building designed by Visconti the Younger and built between 1843 and 1853. One must ascend to the second floor to view the crypt, which is surrounded by a large circular marble wall about a foot wide. Visitors must lean over the wall to see the actual sarcophagus, thus, in effect, bowing to the dead emperor. This is a superb example of using architecture to produce a desired body language.

If you are familiar with body language you know that your movements and posture can affect the people you work with—and vice versa. Try holding your arms across your chest while listening to someone speak and you will convey a sense of being closed to his ideas. Perhaps worse is the person who sits, hands locked behind his head, while leaning back in a chair. Note the proximity of the palms to the ears. This closed-up posture is further compounded by the crossing of feet or legs.

The posture that every salesperson wants to see is the so-called Starter's Position: the client is seated in a relaxed position with feet and hands apart. Try it. First, lean back in your chair with your legs crossed and your hands clasped behind your head. Then, sit on the edge of your chair, feet apart, hands on knees, and lean forward. Don't you feel more receptive?

When I have a sales pitch to make I like to take along a sheet of paper that is about twenty-four inches wide—a graph, a chart, a written proposal, a foldout map—something visual that supports and illustrates the pitch I am making. I sit the width of a desk away from my listener. If I see him assume an undesirable pose, I present the client with the paper in such a way that, in order to reach it, he must uncross his legs, lean forward, and hold the paper with both hands. Almost every time, his body assumes the Starter's Position—and he has unconsciously opened his mind to me while I complete my pitch.

THE MILLION-DOLLAR DOG

Sam was a sales manager at a large corporation and he was having a beastly day. One of his best customers left him, his secretary got exasperated with him, and, of course, the boss was upset over the loss of a valued customer. So Sam dropped the top of his convertible and took the long way home. When passing through a housing development, he saw a little boy sitting on a lawn with a hand-lettered sign that read: Dog for Sale.

Beneath the sign sat a rather scruffy-looking little dog.

Sam pulled over, got out of his car, and walked over to the dog and patted his head. The dog snapped at him.

"What do you want for this gorgeous little dog?" Sam asked the boy.

"A million dollars."

Sam laughed and said, "Now, son, what do you really want for him?"

"I want a million dollars and I won't take a penny less."

The encounter made Sam's day and he drove home in a happy frame of mind.

A couple of months later, wondering what had happened to the little boy and his million-dollar dog, Sam took the same route home. There was the boy sitting on the lawn—but no dog, and no sign.

Sam called the boy over and said, "Son, aren't you the fellow with the million-dollar dog?"

"Yes I am," the boy replied.

"What did you get for him?"

"A million dollars."

"Well, son, I'm a businessman who enjoys complex transactions. Would you take me through the process?"

"It was really easy," answered the boy. "I swapped him for two five-hundred-thousand-dollar cats."

This story was told to me by Meshulem Riklis, the founder and CEO of Rapid America, a conglomerate of hotels and textile companies. He observed that the Harvard Business School method of case studies was an exercise in taphonomy (the study of decay and fossilization). Riklis implied that, by the time a case study is complete, it is already outdated. He considers mergers and acquisitions to be fairly simple and straightforward and used the million-dollar dog to illustrate his point. He then gave two examples.

Riklis was seeking to purchase a textile company in Georgia whose owners were anxious to sell. But when the company had written up the carpets and taken all of the goodwill that it could stand, there was still a million-dollar gap between the price that

Riklis was prepared to pay and the price that the company's management wanted. Riklis asked his vice president to take the company's president for eighteen holes of golf and find out what was troubling him. At the nineteenth hole, the president turned to the vice president and breathlessly said, "Are you really a member of North Augusta? Get me into the club and I'll take a million dollars off the price."

In the other example, a friend of Riklis's father needed to sell his company and Riklis wanted to buy it but, again, there was a million-dollar gap. So a detective was hired to follow the seller for a week. At the end of the week the detective said, "There's really nothing unusual about this guy except that each morning he has a driver with a car pick him up and take him wherever he wants to go." Riklis offered to subsidize this arrangement and the seller took a million dollars off the price.

Riklis was a spellbinding teacher to his fellow presidents in the YPO. One could readily recognize his classroom from the laughter his talks evoked. You might wonder how this applies to other situations. Just remember that most people don't sell something for money; they sell for what the money represents to them. If you can find the right cat, you can often get what you want for less than the asking price. Conceptually, that cat can be taken anywhere.

It's amazing how easy it is to forget this concept. For six years, I had been trying to buy a scenic easement on a farmer's land. He didn't even want to discuss it with me. He just didn't want any encumbrance on his land. Then we found our cat. Noticing that his truck was in a state of collapse, my wife Charlotte told him that our farm needed a new pick-up and asked him to come along and give her some advice. He got a good, close-up view of those shiny new Fords, and a few days later we added a new pick-up truck to our offer for the easement. He accepted. And everybody won.

The farmer held onto a few acres surrounded by a couple hundred acres of cattle-mown lawns. One day his land will be worth a fortune. His son, who continues to live and farm there, will keep the farm for his children. By granting the easement to us, the farmer also drastically reduced the estate tax consequences for his children because farmland is taxed at a far lower rate than developed land. But the tipping point was the shiny new pick-up truck.

The Tipping Point is that magic moment when an idea,
trend or social behavior crosses a threshold, tips, and spreads
like wildfire.

—MALCOLM GLADWELL, The Tipping Point

LESS CAN BE MORE

As the name implies, Hanes Dye and Finishing dyes and finishes cloth. Never one to miss an opportunity, I asked my cousin Gordon Hanes if his company, Hanes Hosiery, had any use for my cloth in his hosiery business. Hanes Hosiery, in fact, bought substantial quantities of cloth which had first to be singed with a hot flame to remove the facial fuzz and then calendared (ironed under several tons of pressure) to make the surface very slick before being made into bags used in dyeing hosiery. I was told it was necessary to treat the cloth in this manner in order to prevent it from snagging the delicate stockings during the tumultuous dyeing procedure.

My cousin gave me some bags to analyze to see if I could come up with a better process. After studying the problem, I reasoned that the way to best prevent snagging would be to leave the fuzz on the cloth and omit the ironing process. So I sent them some bleached material that had been prepared for them, but not yet singed or calendared. The hosiery people loved it, saying that it considerably improved the snagging situation.

I pointed out to their purchasing office that the material was made using the Hanes Dye proprietary "No Snag" finish and sold the new material to them at the same price that they had been paying for the previous dying bags. Ours, of course, were considerably less expensive to produce—a classic example of how less can be more and achieve better results.

LEAVE WELL ENOUGH ALONE

In 1984 Charlotte and I began buying land in a serious way along the New River, which originates in North Carolina and flows north through Virginia and West Virginia to Ohio, where glaciers forced it into the Ohio River. One of the nation's first designated American Heritage Rivers, the New River is the oldest river in the Americas, and geologists estimate that its origins date back more than 320 million years. It is also one of the most ecologically significant river systems in the southern Appalachian Mountains. Beginning with 300 acres I acquired in 1978, Charlotte and I now own over 1,200 acres along the river.

When the local farm agent told us about New Zealand farmers who were, in his opinion, world leaders in producing forage crops, we paid attention. In our region of the state, it makes more sense to concentrate on the quality of forage rather than on the quality of the cattle, because the animals are sold for meat rather than for breeding. So Charlotte and I went to New Zealand, stayed with six farm families during the course of our trip, and ended with a two-day visit to Vaughn Jones, the guru of New Zealand–style intensive rotational grazing.

Two years later Vaughn, with his wife Auriel, came to the United States as a paid consultant and spent three days with us in the mountains. We invited Dr. Vivien Allen, an expert on forages, and Dr. Joe Fontenot, a specialist in cattle management, to join us for dinner at our home in Roaring Gap. The following day we all drove the twenty-two miles to our farm in Virginia, the River Ridge Land and Cattle Company. On the way, Vaughn remarked frequently about the poor appearance of the farms. Finally, Joe Fontenot spoke up, somewhat indignantly, "How dare you criticize our Virginia farms without having set foot on them?"

Vaughn put his arm around Joe and said, soothingly, "When the grass by the side of the road is better than the grass in the pasture, it's a bad farm."

Commenting on the poor appearance of our forage, Vaughn asked our farm manager why he had let it go to seed. The manager answered that heavy rains had turned the soil to mush and he was unable to hay or graze it for fear of "pugging up" the earth.

"Then why didn't you bush hog it (mow it down)?" Vaughn asked.

"What?" replied our manager, "and lose the whole first cutting?"

"Certainly!" said Vaughn. "After it goes to seed it loses most of its nutritional value. Listen, grass has three stages: it lives, it goes to seed, and it dies. If you don't let it go to seed, it will keep on growing; and the hay you make will have tremendous nutritional value."

Since then, if we can't manage the forage because of rain, we cut it down.

Vaughn also asked us why we cut our final hay crop of the season. "Leave it standing. The cattle can feed on it when your pastures have ceased producing forage. They'll do a much more efficient job of harvesting than you will—and think of the time, energy, and equipment you'll save. And,"—he was in full stride by now—"why do you lime once every three years? How deep do you think the roots of grass are? Put down lime every year in far lesser amounts and count your worms. Worms will thrive and are efficient as manure spreaders. They also vastly increase nitrogen content in the soil."

Vaughn's representation of farming practices in New Zealand, especially in its simplicity and more humane treatment of livestock, seemed so obvious—once he had explained them. I asked Vaughn why he didn't spread the word by contributing articles in agricultural publications like *Progressive Farmer* or *Drover Magazine*. He said he had tried, but the magazines' editors feared loss of advertising if they ran such articles.

Modern American agri-business relies on heavy equipment, machinery, and vehicles built by U.S. manufacturers. Our livestock feeds on millions of tons of inefficiently absorbed grains produced by U.S. feed and seed companies. (Because cattle have stomachs that evolved to eat grasses, not grains, commercially produced corn and grain-based feeds are not well-digested and actually deplete healthy omega-3 fats from their meat.) These poorly fed animals are also treated with a dizzying combination of hormones and antibiotics and vaccines, all produced by American pharmaceutical companies. And all of the aforementioned advertise in the ag mags.

Vaughn went on to say that he had met the same obstacles at our universities, which are frequently endowed by corporate generosity. Many of those corporate donors come from agri-business and related industries.

Shortly after Vaughn's visit, I had a long discussion with a retired professor of economics, who derided my argument that finishing cattle on grass was better than trucking them a thousand miles, using tax-subsidized petrol and highways, to feed them on tax-subsidized grain, and that it was less expensive to buy hay than produce it. He countered my newly embraced theories with "evidence" that the American way was to subsidize production with our taxes, and that consumers "benefited" from lower meat prices. He completely dismissed the health drawbacks and denied that the tax subsidies were, in fact, part of the cost.

When I told him that New Zealand-raised lamb and beef and could ship to and sell in America for less than the cost of U.S. products, he asked: "What's wrong with that? I suppose you'd want to stop imports. Should I have to buy a Ford instead of a Mercedes?" This from a university economics professor!

THE CREATIVE PROBLEM SOLVING INSTITUTE

Don't go where the path may lead, go instead where there is no path and make a trail.

—RALPH WALDO EMERSON

Many years ago, even before Madison Avenue became the epicenter of advertising in New York City, Barton, Barton, Durstein and Osborne (BBD&O) was the number-one firm on the street. Its creative soul was Alex Osborne, who lived in Buffalo. On a regular basis one of the partners would board the Buffalo-bound train to meet with Osborne. On one occasion the partner in question told Osborne that he hated the trip and said if Osborne were all that smart, he should be able to teach a young BBD&O associate how to be creative enough to generate the kinds of ideas that would obviate the need for the partners to make this disagreeable journey. Osborne took him seriously and wrote a book, *Creativity*, which is now the textbook for a four-year course at the State University of

New York at Buffalo. The program actually has its own premises, the Creative Problem Solving Institute (CPSI), which the alumni pronounce "sip-see."

Every year in the middle of June, the institute offers a one-week intensive program that anyone can attend. Instructors come from all over the world and there are usually three or four classes for every period. I have taken advantage of these courses three times and have even done a little teaching. I have sent every executive and every supervisor in our corporation to the course and both my wives have attended it.

My first experience at CPSI virtually changed my life. It provided me with a new way of processing and connecting the various events, thoughts, and influences in my daily life. Those first lessons were aimed not only at loosening us up but almost literally returning us to childhood. We were told that, generally speaking, the most creative people are farmers and elementary school teachers. The least creative are the PhDs. For those who might look askance at this, I recommend Michael Lewis's book, *Next: The Future Just Happened,* in which he wrote. "Finland had become the first nation on earth to acknowledge the child-centric model of economic development: if you wanted a fast-growing economy, you needed to promote rapid economic change; and if you intended to promote rapid economic change, you needed to cede to children a strange measure of economic authority." He goes on to tell of two fifteen-year-olds, one of whom was the first minor charged with stock-market fraud and the other who pretended to have a law degree and became so adept that lawyers across the country were consulting him.

I can honestly say that first session can change your whole life. The courses are fascinating. I remember in particular a course called "How to Invent an Artificial Kidney" and another one "How I Invented the Plastic Shotgun Shell." The latter was especially interesting. The inventor worked for either Winchester or Remington, I can't remember which. Called to an executive meeting, he was informed that the research and development lab had at last delivered a plastic that could withstand the explosion of a shotgun shell. When asked if he could invent a machine that would produce a large quantity of shells per hour, he thought about it for a few minutes and said he could. When asked how long it would take, as I recall, he said about nine months. How much would it cost? He named a rather large figure, explaining that he needed a large hydraulic ram that could easily power two machines, not just one, because it would be more cost effective to proceed with two. When asked if he could produce the machine, he responded "absolutely." He left the meeting and went to his office where he ordered a very expensive hydraulic ram.

"Had he," I asked, "already completely invented the machine in his mind?"

"Not at all," said the instructor. "I just knew that I could." To free up his mind, he went out and played eighteen holes of golf. In due course he produced the machine in less time than he had estimated and under budget. The critical element was the absolute necessity of relaxing and getting his mind off a complex problem's potential solution. He had faith that the solution would come.

I learned a few other useful principles and ploys during my stints at CPSI. For instance, I learned to keep my eyes open for opportunities to take a problem and turn it upside down, make it smaller or larger, reverse it, break it into many parts, turn it inside out, or do something absolutely foolish with it—the first wild thought that pops into my mind. (This last is especially productive when brainstorming with a group.)

START AT THE END

Sometimes, you can take this suggestion absolutely literally. Back in the 1920s there was a great pianist named Vladimir de Pachmann. Audiences loved him, but the critics were less enthusiastic. They said he was too much of a showman. He liked to make a great production of his entrance and acknowledge the applause with exaggerated bows. Then he would pause dramatically before flinging the tails of his swallow-tail coat with a dramatic sweep of his hand before sitting down to play. During a performance, he often mirrored the drama of the music by emoting with facial expressions that ranged from beatific smiles to angry scowls. A shameless flirt, he loved to wink at the ladies in the front row.

During one season, a performance was announced before he had thoroughly rehearsed two of the pieces listed on his program. When playing the first, a Chopin prelude, he noticed that at a particular phrase in the music, while concentrating on just the right facial expression or gesture, he missed a measure and landed back at the beginning of the piece. The first performance was coming up in Cincinnati. As preparations were made for de Pachmann's entrance, he asked the stage manager to place the sheet music on the piano upside down.

That evening, de Pachmann strode to the piano. With a look of abject horror on his face, he turned to the audience. "Music? Music for de Pachmann? De Pachmann never use music!" Then he paused and smiled, "Ah, now I know! Cincinnati is such a friendly city, such a kind city. Everywhere I go in your city, people smile at me and say hello. Everyone is so nice. Your stage manager, he's so nice. He saw this music in my dressing room and he put it here for me. So kind, so thoughtful! So tonight, de Pachmann make history. De Pachmann will use music."

"But," he said, with a knowing smile to the audience, "I will turn it upside down!"

FOLLOW THE LEADER

While living in London at the behest of the Navy during the Korean War, I had the good fortune to find a kindred soul in my fellow lieutenant, Harry Joyce, who joined me in learning about French wines. We became enthusiastic oenophiles.

When we returned to the States, the Joyces invited my wife and I to Linville, North Carolina, for the weekend. We arrived late, were handed a glass of sherry, and taken straight into the dining room for a seven-course meal. When the fish course arrived, Harry's maid brought in a bottle wrapped in a napkin.

I said, "Harry, I can't wait to taste this Graves."

"How do you know it's a Graves?"

I replied. "Any disciple of Brillat-Savarin would prefer Graves with sole véronique."

Throughout the meal, Harry puzzled over this. Finally he said, "Damn it, Phil, I can think of several wines I could have served just as well as the Graves. How in the hell did you know which one it was?"

"I could see the shape of the bottle," I explained. Hipped bottles are Bordeaux and sloped bottles are Burgundies. The only French

Bordeaux generally sold in the United States in the 1950s were sweet dessert wines such as Château d'Yquem and a Château Latour Blanc—except for Graves.

When we returned to Winston-Salem from London, I found the only wines available in my hometown were sherry, vermouth, port, and Mogen David. What to do but organize a strategy to change the situation? So I persuaded ten members of the Old Town Club to form a wine club within the club. We each put up $50 and with that we bought several cases of four wines—Beaujolais, St-Émilion, Chablis, and Pouilly-Fuissé (or Pully Fussy, as my friends called it). In those days, a twelve-bottle case of Beaujolais cost around $10. When the wines arrived, a wine list with the Old Town Club logo was printed. Brandishing my new wine list, I informed my friends at the nearby Forsyth Country Club that, unless they wanted to appear uncosmopolitan, they too should have their own stock of wine. Pretty soon, that club had its own list.

With two lists in hand, I went to see Mary Chamis, who ran two local restaurants, Steak House One and Steak House Two. She was obviously impressed with the lists, but said she doubted if many of her clients would be interested. I told her to get two cases of each and print up a wine list. I promised to buy back any wine left at year's end. Armed with the restaurant lists and club lists, I hit Lawrence Staley's restaurant. It was an easy mark, and by the end of the year you could buy good wine all over town.

In 1959, when Charles Mark was the director of Winston-Salem's Arts Council (the first arts council in the nation), he and I formed the Tri-States Arts Council, which brought together North Carolina, South Carolina, and Virginia. In 1965, when New York chartered the first state arts council, its chairman, John McFadyen, visited us for two days to discuss the background and history of arts councils. McFadyen was a well-known architect and man-about-town in New York City and I wanted to impress him. The only restaurant we could brag about back then was Staley's, which had superb steak. I suggested that, being from New York, he had probably enjoyed a surfeit of French and Italian food, so I would take him to a fine local restaurant for a really great piece of meat as a change of pace.

"No need to bring the wine list," I told my favorite waitress, "that Beaujolais will be just right." I knew the list included only four wines, plus I didn't want to give her the chance to say "Boo-jo-lay."

She poured a small amount of the wine in my glass, and then, before I could taste it, she filled the glass.

"Aw heck, Mr. Hanes," she said. "You don't have to taste it. I served this wine to you last week." John never let me forget this.

IN THE BUFF: A TRILOGY

1. Don't Knock the Competition

When I was a salesman for Hanes Dye and Finishing Company, I often spent lonely evenings in small hotel rooms thumbing through the Yellow Pages looking for ideas about who might need their cloth dyed. Thus it was that in Chicago I saw an entry for Buffing Wheels. Knowing that buffing wheels are mostly made from cloth, I pressed a call on the American Buffing Wheel Company, hopeful that they might need our services.

The owner, Leonard Sax, was not overly busy and gave me a liberal education in buffing and polishing. I learned that buffing "bright work," such as chrome-plated automobile bumpers, was a function of speed, pressure, the density of the buff cloth, and head (the amount of fine grit in a stick of the high–melting-point wax that is applied to the wheel). "It's an art more than a science," he explained.

Most buffing wheels are made with many layers of cloth held together by two connected metal discs. In the days when prices were controlled by the government, specifically, the Office of Price Administration (OPA), the cost of a regulated item could not be increased unless there was something new about it. So buffing wheel manufacturers dyed their material a maize color. Much to their surprise, the wheels polished more of whatever it was that they were polishing. So the manufacturers that used huge ranges (rows of buffing wheels) found it less expensive to pay a higher price for the "new" yellow wheels. Time and labor was saved because depleted buffing ranges were dismantled and replaced less often. What caused the greater longevity of the cloth? Apparently, the hot water used during the dyeing process tended to spread the starch already imbedded in the warp threads more evenly throughout the fabric, thus creating a tougher material. Sax told me that the same two textile finishers in New Jersey had been treating cloth for him since the OPA regulations were established. They were excellent, efficient suppliers, who dyed his cloth in quantity for two cents a yard. He conceded that he liked me, but that two cents a yard on a wheel costing several dollars was so insignificant to him that he would not consider switching to a brand-new supplier—even though he often had up to 50,000 yards of material dyed at a time.

For the life of me I could not see how we could profit from such a low-cost process, but I thought it was worth a shot. Shortly afterward, still in pursuit of the buffing wheel business, I called on George Churchill Buffing located in Hingham, Massachusetts. Mr.

Churchill was kind enough to agree to let us finish a small 2,000-yard lot of fabric for him. We gave it our best shot, but the process cost us more than two cents a yard and we realized that, even in larger quantities, the business would yield only a slight profit. When we returned the cloth to Mr. Churchill, he complained about the length of time the job had taken, "two weeks is no good"; and he was aghast that we returned to him $2^1/2$ percent more material than he had sent us.

"I get overnight delivery and a 100-percent return—I don't want you stretching my cloth," he said. I explained that it was nearly impossible to treat the cloth in a day and that because the cloth shrinks when it's wet, the process of returning the cloth to its original width caused unavoidable stretching in length. He did not believe me.

Now I knew where the profits in this business were. His suppliers were subtracting the known gain (probably a bolt or two) from each lot until they accumulated a sizeable quantity, which they dyed and kept in their own inventory. When the customer sent them an order, they substituted material from this hodge-podge of already dyed stock and thus could offer overnight delivery. Many buffing wheel manufacturers were paying a premium for a special quality cloth from Deering Milliken, and they were not getting back the same cloth they had delivered for processing. The dyers were making their profit by selling already finished fabric. This looked like fun!

On my next visit to the area, I found George as friendly as ever and slightly amused that I had come back. During our conversation, I found out that his largest customer was the Ternstedt Plant of the Ford Motor Company. When Churchill called on the plant's purchasing agent, he had to pass between long rows of buffing ranges. When I questioned him, George said the purchasing agent told him that Churchill Buffing was getting 25 percent of the plant's business. I asked George if he believed it. "No!" was George's emphatic response.

So I said to him, "You fellows in the business tell me that buffing is an art, not a science. Therefore, it seems to me that the guy on the buff range sees himself as the artist. How would you like to try out a little art here? I'll make up a color card for you, and we'll confine one of the colors to you. Then when you walk down the ranges at the Ford plant, you can count how many wheels have your color. Tell the purchasing agent to tell the men that this is a new, improved treatment."

I persuaded two other buffing wheel manufacturers who also sold to Ford to do the same. All liked the idea, especially as the new color could, as an "improvement," command a higher price. I gave them the dye formula to check with their current finishing companies, all of which said, "No problem!"—that is, until they came to the part about overnight delivery.

"Sorry. It will take at least two-and-a-half weeks to process cloth to these specifications," they said. All of a sudden, not only was overnight delivery impossible, but also the turnaround time would be longer than ours. The word spread quickly about what the other vendors had been doing. They were thus hoist on their own petard and we won all of Ford's business almost overnight. And I never said a word.

What are the two points to this story?

Number #1: Don't knock your competitors—if you can defeat them without their realizing what you are up.

Number #2: You can develop an effective game plan if you ask enough of the right questions.

2. Price as a Disguise

After George Churchill became a loyal customer, I said to him, "We've seen that the introduction of a new buff color seems to get good results. We know that it's vital for the buffing wheel to hold its head (the wax-encased grit applied to it). What if we introduced some high–melting-point wax to the treatment and told the purchasing agent to tell his operators that we think this buff will hold its head better?" He agreed to try and the plan was successful enough that we both made a little extra change. We called it the Hanes Waxbuff.

Meanwhile, there was a fire in the buffing range exhausts at the Ternstedt Plant (where Ford polished most of its car bumpers) that had severely damaged the plant. Such fires were common, but this one got out of hand. I told George Churchill we could give him a fire-retardant cloth that would solve the problem. Our first attempt to produce the material was a dismal failure—it simply fell apart when heated. After months of experimenting, we found a very expensive product that we combined with our Waxbuff treatment, and it did the job to Ford's liking.

A year later, I asked our finishing department to try a small lot using the cheapest fire-retardant on the market to combine with the wax. We were amazed—it did an even better job! George was also delighted because the "new, improved Hanes Fyrwax" would cost him the same as the old, even though he was able to charge a bit more for it.

Months later our chairman called me in and said, "I have been reviewing our products and noticed that, although the quantities of buff cloth we're selling are small, we're making a lot of profit. Congratulations! But, in a business where a 3- to 5-percent profit is OK, 250 percent on that Fyrwax treatment is unheard of. We must lower the price or we might lose the business to our competition."

I asked if we could patent the process. He said, "No, the formula could easily be duplicated using a different mix." I pointed out that its simplicity made it easy to analyze. However, "everybody knows" in our industry that you cannot make a 250-percent profit. He didn't think much of my reasoning, but as I had built the business, he let it be.

A year later I was attending a meeting of the Textile Chemists and Colorists when the chief scientist of a competitive finishing company, Deering Milliken, approached me and said, "I want to congratulate you on that Fyrwax formula. We had our whole lab force analyze it and all we can find is two common inexpensive salts and a high–melting-point wax. You've discovered something inert that we can't find."

And I said, "No, and you never will."

3. Blue-Collar Art

As you will remember, "buffing is more of an art than a science." So, once more, after our adventures with color changes and fire-retardants, I asked the always-game George Churchill if he'd like try another incursion into the world of "art."

I pointed out that abrasive wheels were heavy-duty wheels designed to cut deeply into metal and that they have a reputation for being very tough. I dyed two samples of buffing material—one in taupe brown (I suggested the brown because psychologists say it represents stability and dependability) and the other in the battleship gray that was common to the abrasive wheels of the day. I suggested that we put a healthy price on our treatment and that George increase his wheel price also.

We registered the name Tuffbuff so that we could add that cute little®. Tuffbuff® made it appear that we had made a proprietary advance in technology. I promised George a one-year exclusivity.

George showed our product to an operator whom he knew personally, told him that he was giving the company some wheels with the new Tuffbuff® treatment, and he had chosen his friend to do the big test. The results were marvelous and we sold a lot of treatment for the heavy-duty wheels. We discovered that buffing really is an art—and both George and I sold our art—and profited accordingly.

> *I work in wood because of its transparent, reflecting qualities that enhance an illusionary sense. One of my greatest pleasures was serving a dinner at a table that did not exist. Sanded and polished, wood allows for a repetition of line, texture and surface color which creates a graphic rhythm. My addition of metal and industrial parts contributes to the clean contemporary look, and can also work structurally to enhance both the scale and the price.*

—GARRY KNOX BENNETT, Made in Oakland

UP FRONT VERSUS
THE BOTTOM LINE

Many go fishing all their lives without knowing
that it is not the fish they are after.

—HENRY DAVID THOREAU

The bottom line is the important one, but it is also important to realize that the arithmetic can be quite subtle. Job applicants often place more weight on salary in their determination to achieve the highest take-home after-tax income, and in doing so miss out on other benefits.

When Robert Ward, then chancellor of the North Carolina School of the Arts, decided to give up administrative work so he could return to composing, we brought in a candidate who had been dean of music at a large university. At the end of the interview he said he liked the school very much and would be interested in the job. But, when we told him the position's salary, he asked how dare we fly him all the way across the country and take up his time for such a pittance? So we told him.

First, we asked him who owned his house. He said he had a mortgage on it, plus all the upkeep, repairs, and grounds maintenance. We asked him who equipped the house with appliances—dishwasher, refrigerator, stove, and so on—and handled the repairs. He did. He also had a car loan, plus the expense of tires, oil, gas, servicing, and washing. He employed a housekeeper who cleaned once a week. Added to this were newspaper and magazine subscriptions. Then, of course, he took (and paid for) an annual vacation. An accountant was called in to put pencil to paper and add up the candidates current living expenses.

By contrast, the North Carolina School of the Arts had provided Robert Ward with a house and a studio over the garage. The house was furnished, with kitchen and laundry appliances included. The school also gave him a car and took care of all the associated expenses. It provided a housekeeper and a groundskeeper, and even covered most of his magazines and newspapers, which Robert turned over to the school's reception room after he had finished with them. Robert also had an expense account. Various members of the school board often offered him a vacation site, thus drastically reducing his vacation costs. The reader won't be surprised to learn that Bob Ward's take-home pay was actually higher than what the candidate was left with at the end of very month. We were not surprised either, but the candidate was.

There are many ways for an executive of a nonprofit organization to enjoy similar benefits. Just look around.

- A house can be a gift from an estate (consult bankers, trust lawyers, realtors, etc.).

- Money for the purchase of a house can come from a foundation or business if the name of the business is in some way associated with the house, or if the foundation can rent it out in what amounts to pre-tax dollars to the applicant, rather than paying for a house in after-tax dollars.

- Furnishings and equipment can be supplied, using similar arrangements, by manufacturers and/or retailers with unsold inventory.

- A car can be a gift from a dealer or manufacturer; it can be bought or leased with pre-tax dollars; a used car from a corporation's fleet can also be received as a gift.

- Staff support (groundskeepers/maintenance workers) can come from your own organization's staff.

- Periodicals can be supplied as gifts from the newspaper or magazine distributors; or the organization itself can pay for the publications desired by the institution.

- Education benefits for the children are especially easily arranged in an educational institution.

- Vacation sites can often be obtained from friends of the institution or board members, who may themselves be eligible to take tax deductions if they already rent out their property.

- Finally, it can be very helpful if you can offer a good job for the spouse. This can be the deal-maker.

Of course, this all transpired many years ago. Be sure to contact your tax advisor regarding current tax laws.

MAY I HAVE YOUR ATTENTION, PLEASE?

Most people love to talk, but hate to make speeches. Nevertheless, speech making is a vital tool for selling yourself, an idea, or a project. And you have to speak up if you're going to network or persuade folks to do what needs to be done.

When Admiral Tip Merrill's wife was invited to make a speech to the annual meeting of the Red Cross, she asked her husband to compose the address for her. She gave him several months to accomplish this task, pressing him often about his progress. The speech would be ready in plenty of time, he assured her. As the day drew closer, and there was no sign of a speech, Mrs. Merrill grew alarmed. On the day before the speech, her husband handed her an elaborately wrapped package. She opened it to find a brass doorknob.

"Hold on to this, my dear," he told her, "and you will have no problem."

Said Mrs. Merrill, "I could have killed him!"

All the brass doorknobs in the world won't substitute for careful preparation. Know what you want to say before you have to stand up and say it. Some of the best advice on public speaking came from a country preacher who said, "First, tell 'em what you're gonna tell 'em. Then tell 'em. Then tell' em what you told 'em." In other words, give a clear, short introduction or overview. Deliver the speech. Then summarize—briefly—and wrap it up.

I feel that I am a wooden speaker if I have to walk up to a podium and face an audience of strangers. It always helps if I've had a chance to socialize a bit beforehand.

One way to put your audience—and yourself—at ease is to have fun with the introduction. In response to a flowery introduction, I like to recite this ditty:

■ ■ ■

WHEN I AM PRAISED FOR WORK I'VE DONE

I DEPRECATE SUCH FLATTERY, PRETEND IT'S A BORE.

I TURN ASIDE BACK-SLAPPING FRIENDS,
ENCOMIUMS DEPLORE.

BUT DEEP INSIDE MY FAKING HEART I'M CHANTING,
"MORE, MORE, MORE."

■ ■ ■

Or, as Ernest Hemingway said, "You finally reach the shore and the bastards hit you over the head with a life belt."

Recently, as I was preparing to make an acceptance speech for a service award, I told my partner Chris Griffith I didn't know which was worse—having stage fright or worrying about being overly emotional when I received the award. Chris suggested that I simply look at the audience and picture them sitting there naked.

So I said, "I was fearful of getting moist around the eyes over such an honor as this. Chris Griffith suggested that I look out at you and visualize you all being naked. So I did—and now I really feel like crying." They laughed at me and I laughed at their reaction.

■ ■ ■

My own tips for speech making are short and few, but they are effective:

- Be succinct—no longer than twenty minutes, unless you have visuals that require perusal rather than a glance.

- Use visuals when possible; your audience will pay closer attention and will remember more of what you have to say if you involve two or more of their senses.

- Tell your audience what you're going to say, say it, and then tell them what you said.

- Involve your audience. Nothing keeps their attention better than asking them a question that requires a response. For instance: "Can you hear me all right? Does that apply to you folks in the back row? (Those folks may be intentionally sitting near the exit.)"

"Am I mumbling? If so, raise a hand."

"Am I going too fast? Are you following me thus far? Does someone need a clarification?"

If you start your audience off with a laugh, you'll relax them. If you engage them, you will retain their attention. Keep it short and repeat your message, and there's a good chance your address has a future.

DEC?DING THE RÉSUMÉ

Many résumés are written by experts in obfuscation. The candidate always appears to be ideally suited for the job. Few employers have experience with interviewing and their simplistic questions offer too much latitude to the wily candidate. The really useful (personal) questions—marital status, health, finances, among others—are precluded by law. So it takes work to reveal the information one truly needs to know about a candidate's aptitude to fill a particular position over the long haul.

I first found the need for a good method of judging applicants for managerial positions when I took over the presidency of our manufacturing company in 1958. I wanted an interview format that would give me clear indicators of a candidate's direction and motivation, as well as evidence of perseverance, evasiveness, creativity, aggressiveness, decisiveness, and so on. I sought interview questions from business schools at the University of North Carolina, Harvard, Wharton, Stanford, and others. I was surprised when none of them could suggest a framework for a comprehensive interrogation. Could this be because it is assumed that someone else has already asked the hard questions?

Most organizations seeking an executive will engage a head-hunting firm and assume they'll screen the candidates with an incisive interview before dispatching the beautifully presented résumé and cover letter. Then the candidate is reviewed by a director for human resources and invited to meetings or to meals with board members and peer groups. The finalists are invited, together with a spouse, to a social event. If no hideous social gaffes are perpetrated, a marked appetite for alcohol is not apparent, and the general appearance seems acceptable, the candidate is hired.

Recently, a major arts institution in Winston-Salem hired a so-called nationally recognized search firm to fill a crucial top management position. Of the two finalists, only one had enough personal interest in the arts to attend any consequential performances, programs, or exhibitions. Clearly the head-hunter's primary interview was deficient and early interviews at the institution itself failed to reveal this anomaly. Only our interview revealed the candidates' real interests—or lack of them.

To me, the accepted standard process seems both protracted and inconclusive. So I have developed my own interview, which can take over two hours, but can chase a rat out of its hole, if rats there be. First, review the résumé carefully to help you focus each question. After no more than an exchange of names, inform the candidate that this is a standard list of questions asked of all applicants for the job. Then, begin the interview immediately.

The interview is designed to be given by one person to the final aspirants before the final decision-makers meet the candidates. It consists of three elements: a series of questions (there are forty-six of them, which is why two hours may be required, and they are, intentionally, in no particular order), and two checklists that are reviewed by the interviewer after the question-and-answer session. In preparation, I print out the questions and leave enough space below each (approximately $1^1/2$ inches) for jotting down responses and noting body language (for example, "fidgets," or "hesitant; lots of ums and uhs").

Some of the questions are tough—and they're supposed to be. If you want a true picture of the candidate, don't skip any. For example, Question 24: "What has stopped you from getting ahead more quickly?" takes nerve to ask, but often elicits a revealing response. I ask it of everyone, regardless of age or status. Interestingly, only once in dozens of interviews has a respondent been satisfied with his progress.

Sometimes during an interview, I am asked to explain or elaborate, to which I say, "Just put your own spin on it." This response puts the ball back into the candidate's court and saves me from expressing my bias, favorable or unfavorable. This is especially true of the final

Question 46: "Tell me a story." It often provokes a counter question: "What kind of story?" I invariably respond, "You decide." Here one is likely to get either a very creative tale, or the candidate uses the story to tell you something about herself you might have missed in the questioning.

I conducted just such an interview with the British drama professor Malcolm Morrison, who was a candidate for dean of drama at the North Carolina School of the Arts. As the interview progressed, he became more and more irate. When I asked the final question, he replied, "I will NOT tell you a damned story!"

I coughed and said, "Well, that's all the questions there are. Let's go have a beer." I had found his flash point and, although he wanted the job, he had had enough and said so. He went on to become one of our most effective deans.

When the interview questions are complete, I adopt a more relaxed, conversational tone and then we review the résumé together. I focus in particular on responses to queries that my interview suggests will need further elaboration.

After the interview, I run down the checklists, one of which addresses aspects of personality, the other aspects of behavior, and add my comments. The questions and answers are then entered into a database. I find it helpful to go over the candidate's responses, highlighting in red those I find detrimental and using blue for those that seem to be on target. In my review, I pay particular attention to repetition. One candidate, for example, frequently mentioned his strong religious convictions and said that he spent a lot of time with fellow employees "convincing them of the right way to do things." When highlighted, these and other remarks about attention to detail and so forth indicated a fairly hide-bound individual who was set in his ways and might be averse to the kinds of creative approaches required by the job in question.

The R. Philip Hanes Interview

Instructions for giving this interview: Thoroughly familiarize yourself with the résumé. Do not exchange pleasantries before the interview. Simply say, "This is a standard interview we give to every-one. Do you mind if I take notes?" Then write down the answers to the questions, noting the body language as well ("Looked stumped," or "Long hesitation," or "Nervous; seemed evasive"). When asked to interpret or expand on a question, simply say: "Just put your own spin on it."

When you are finished, write up the interview for perusal by others.

THE QUESTIONNAIRE

1. Why do you think you might like to work for this company (organization)?

2. Do you know anything about arts management?

3. What college did you attend? What degree did you earn?

4. What subjects did you enjoy?

5. In what school activities did you participate? Why? Which did you enjoy most?

6. How do you spend your spare time? What are your hobbies?

7. In what position in the company are you most interested?

8. What starting salary would you expect?

9. Have you traveled much? Where?

10. Would you mind a job that required traveling?

11. What progress in our organization would seem normal to you?

12. What would you say are your best qualities?

13. How would you sell or promote our product (activities)? What would you say constitutes a good sales approach?

14. What are your computer proficiencies?

15. What did you particularly like about your last job? Dislike?

16. What would you like to have done more of in your last job?

17. What suggestion did you make to improve operations or morale?

18. What was your best boss like? Your worst boss?

19. What should management do to assist you in this position?

20. Why do you think you were a valuable employee?

21. What makes the difference between success and failure?

22. What was the most difficult thing you ever tackled? The most gratifying?

23. What do people usually criticize you for? What do you criticize them for?

24. What has stopped you from getting ahead more quickly?

25. Why do you think you would be good at this job?

26. If hired, how would you picture your future here?

27. How does this job compare with others you have applied for?

28. If you could have had any career, what would it have been? Why?

29. Why did you choose your particular field of work?

30. How did you spend your vacations while at school?

31. What do you know about this organization:

    —its direction and history?

    —its staff?

    —its board?

32. Do you think your extracurricular activities in college were worth the time you devoted to them? Why?

33. How did previous employers treat you?

34. What have you learned from some of the jobs you have held?

35. Are you eager to please?

36. How do you usually spend weekends?

37. Is it an effort for you to be tolerant of people with a background and interests different from your own?

38. What types of books have you read?

39. How often do you entertain at home?

40. What have you done that shows initiative and willingness to work?

41. Do you wish to be a leader? Why? How?

42. What sort of housing will you require?

43. What do you know of this town? What do you like most about it?

44. Where do you eventually hope to settle?

45. When do you like to take vacations? How long?

46. Tell me a story.

Checklist #1: Personality

The preceding questions address various aspects of personality and, when the answers are taken in the aggregate and considered in light of others in that group, they can indicate specific and differing aspects of the candidate's personality and attitudes:

___ Primary desire for money (see questions 1, 7, 8, 11, 20, 26)

___ Knowledge of the organization (see questions 1, 26, 27, 31)

___ Diversity of interests (see question 4)

___ Friendliness and energy level (see questions 5, 32, 33, 35, 37)

___ Breadth of interests (see questions 6, 9, 30, 38)

___ A mover and shaker (see questions 11, 13)

___ A desire to travel/possibly good in sales, poor in a desk job (see questions 9, 30)

___ Significant personality traits (see questions 12, 23)

___ Creativity (see questions 13, 17, 19, 30, 46)

___ Compatibility with fellow employees (see questions 15, 17, 18, 33, 40)

___ Possibly overlooked good qualities/braggart? (see questions 20, 25)

___ Achievement orientation (see question 21)

___ Unusual responses (see question 24)

___ Evidence of dissatisfaction with career (see questions 28, 29)

___ A "yes" man (see question 35)

___ Ascertains religious fervor and family involvement (see question 36)

___ Aggressiveness, ambition (see question 41)

Checklist #2: Behavior

When the interview is complete, review your impressions and check off instances of the behavior traits listed on page 160.

___ Overbearing (overaggressive, conceited, exhibiting a superiority complex; a know-it-all)

___ Inability to express self clearly (poor voice, diction, grammar)

___ Lack of planning for career (no purpose or goals)

___ Lack of interest and enthusiasm (passive, indifferent)

___ Lack of confidence and poise (nervousness, ill at ease)

___ Failure to participate in activities

___ Overemphasis on money (interested only in best-dollar offer)

___ Poor scholastic record (just got by)

___ Unwilling to start at bottom (expects too much too soon)

___ Makes excuses, evasive

___ Lack of tact

___ Lack of maturity

___ Lack of courtesy (ill-mannered)

___ Critical of past employers

___ Lack of awareness of the social niceties

___ Marked dislike for school work

___ Lack of vitality

___ Fails to look interviewer in the eye

___ Limp, fishy handshake

___ Indecision

___ Loafs during vacations (lakeside pleasures)

___ Unhappy married life

___ Sloppy application form

___ Merely shopping around

___ Wants job for only a short time

___ Little sense of humor

___ Lack of knowledge of field of specialization

___ Parents make decisions for him or her

___ No interest in company or industry

___ Emphasis on whom he knows

___ Unwillingness to go where we send him or her

___ Cynical

___ Low moral standards

___ Lazy

___ Intolerant, strong prejudices

___ Narrow interests

___ Spends much time watching television

___ Poor handling of personal finances

___ No interest in community activities

___ Inability to take criticism

___ Radical ideas

APPENDIX II

CURRICULUM VITAE

ARTS—International

Arts International Magazine founding board member, 1981–1985

International Council of the Museum of Modern Art, board member, 1978–1994

International Committee of the New York City Ballet, board member, 1984–1986

Salzburg Seminar in American Studies, board member, Development Committee, 1978–1982; Senior Fellow, 1997

Spoleto Festival, board member, Development Committee, 1979–1993

ARTS—National / Public

National Cultural Center, appointed by President Kennedy, board member, 1962–1965

National Endowment for the Arts, appointed by President Johnson, charter board member Music Panel, 1965–1972

Kennedy Center for the Performing Arts, appointed by President Ford, board member; director Finance Committee, 1975–1979; Friends of the Kennedy Center, trustee emeritus

Smithsonian American Art Museum, board member; chairman, Development Committee, 1976; Renwick Gallery, board member, 1976–1988; Advisory Committee, 1988–

Business Committee for the Arts, board member, 1976–1986

Alliance for Arts Education, board member, 1976–1979

National Council for Arts and Education, Executive Committee, 1976–1979

National Council of the Arts, Music Panel, 1972–1974

Federal Reserve Bank of Washington, D.C., Fine Arts Committee, Nominating Committee, 1979–1981

Federal Reserve Bank of Richmond, Va., Advisory Council on Arts, 1977–1978

American Art Forum, Washington, D.C., founder/chairman, 1986–1988

Ambassadors for the Arts, NEA, Executive Committee, 1999–

ARTS—National / Private

American Symphony Orchestra League, charter board member, Convention and Development committees, 1958–1961

American Council for the Arts (now Americans for the Arts), founder, vice president, president, 1960–1969; Development and Nominations committees; chairman Convention Committee

National Association of Local Arts Agencies, founded in my living room, 1971

American Crafts Council, National Advisory Committee, 1970–1972

American Heritage Dance Theatre (Agnes de Mille), founding board member, 1972–1975

Pauline Koner Dance Consort, Advisory Board, 1977–1985

Performing Arts Review, consulting editor, 1981–1986

Journal of Arts Management and Law, consulting editor, 1981–1986

Art Economist, Editorial Advisory Board, 1982–1986

Penland School of Crafts, Inc., Advisor on Development, 1960–1979; Honorary Board of Trustees, 1988–

Jargon Society, president Development Committee, 1968–1999

Winterthur Museum, board member Development Committee, 1972–1977

Walpole Society, board member, 1970–1984

Pennsylvania Academy of Fine Arts, life fellow, 1972–

Yale University, founder, chairman Committee on Music, 1970–1973; Jonathan Edwards College, associate fellow, 1971–1974

Tri-States Arts Council (Va., S.C., N.C.), founder, chairman of the board, 1959–1961

Barter Theater (State Theater of Virginia), Board of Visitors, 1967–1975

Brevard School of Music, Board of Visitors, 1969–1974

Cornell University, Graduate School of Business, Arts Administration Division, Advisory Council, 1980–1981

Arena Stage, Board of Directors, Development, 1989–1992

ARTS—State / Public

Conservatory Investigation Committee (mayor's appointment), founder, chairman, 1963–1964

North Carolina School of the Arts, appointed by Governor Sanford, founder, board member, 1966–1978

Moore, Scott, Holshouser and Hunt, Nominating, Development, Executive committees; chairman, '63 Fund Drive; founder, Board of Visitors

Roger L. Stevens Center for the Performing Arts, chairman, Fund Drive, 1978–1987

North Carolina Dance Theater, board development, public relations, 1978–1981

North Carolina State Arts Council, appointed by Governor Sanford, founder, chairman, Executive Committee, 1964–1967

Governor's Council on Business, Arts, and Humanities, appointed by Governor Hunt, founder, board member, Development Committee, 1977–1986

Stevens Center Community Council, founder, chairman, 1989–

ARTS—Local

Piedmont Festival, board member, 1949–1950

Southeastern Center for Contemporary Art (SECCA), founder, board member, 1956–1958; Development and Nominating committees

Moravian Music Foundation, board member, 1963–1965

Winston-Salem Arts Council, founder, board member, vice president, 1949, 1953–1964; Personnel, Nominating, Development, Executive, Endowment, and Long-Range Planning Committees

Winston-Salem Symphony, board member, Development Committee, 1955–1956

Little Theater, board member, Nominating and Development Committee, 1958–1961

Arts and Crafts Association, board member, 1958–1961

Film Friends, board member, 1960–1962

Piedmont Opera, founder, vice president, board member, 1958–1961

Salem College, board member, chairman Arts Center Fund Drive, 1961–1964

WFDD-FM (National Public Radio), board member, 1978–1980

Art Based Elementary School, board member, 2000

Winston-Salem Commission of Cultural Affairs, founder, commissioner, 2001–

Mint Museum (Charlotte, N.C.) Craft Advisory Committee, 2004–

ARTS CONSULTANT

Salzburg Seminars in American Studies, Salzburg, Austria, 1978

Government of Austria, 1978

Government of Puerto Rico, 1978

San Antonio, Texas, 1978

Walnut Street Theatre, Philadelphia, 1983

Roanoke: The Voyages of John White (3-hour TV series), 1984

AWARDS

Junior Chamber of Commerce, Young Man of the Year—Winston-Salem, N.C., 1958

Junior Chamber of Commerce, Young Man of the Year—North Carolina, 1958

Winston-Salem Arts Council Award, 1960

National Endowment of the Arts, Chairman's Award, 1966

North Carolina Public Service Award, 1976

Morrison Award for the Arts (N.C.), 1977

Swan Award (Tenn.), 1979

North Carolina Society of New York Award, 1979

Community Service Award, Winston-Salem Urban League, 1979

National Governor's Association Award for Distinguished Service to the Arts, 1982

North Carolina Award in Fine Arts, 1982

Winston-Salem NAACP Award (two awards), 1983

Mule Collar Award–Yale University, Class of '49, 1983

National Medal of Arts (presented by President Bush), 1991

Piedmont Opera Theatre Award, 1992

Giannini Award (North Carolina School of the Arts), 1994

National Arts Club Tribute, New York City, 1995

Southeastern Center for Contemporary Art (SECCA), Leadership in the Arts Award, 1998

Charlotte and Philip Hanes Art Gallery, Wake Forest University, 2001

Lifetime Achievement Award, *Winston-Salem Chronicle*, 2002

Downtown Winston-Salem Excellence Award, 2003

Charlotte and Philip Hanes Student Commons Building, North
Carolina School of the Arts, 2003

Winston-Foundation Award, 2003

National Association of State Arts Agencies Founder Award, 2005

LHD, St. Andrews Presbyterian College, Laurinberg, N.C., 1981

DFA, North Carolina School of the Arts, Winston-Salem, N.C., 1987

HHD, Wake Forest University, Winston-Salem, N.C., 1990

AWARDS as CEO of Hanes Companies

Business Committee for the Arts, 1966, 1968, 1971, 1975, 1979, 1981

North Carolina Governor's Award in the Arts and Humanities, 1985

CONSERVATION ORGANIZATIONS

North Carolina Recreation Committee, member, 1962–1965

Stone Mountain Park and Preservation Committee, founder and vice
chairman, 1968–1974

Appalachian Trail Conference, national advisor, 1973–1976

National Audubon Society, board member; Development, Nominating,
and Business Relations committees, 1972–1978

Isaac Walton League of America, board member, founder Board of
Trustees, Nominating and Development committees, 1974–1978

Nature Conservancy, board member, Development, Land Acquisition,
Nominating, and Corporate Relations committees, 1975–1979

American Land Trust, board member, 1976–1984

Appalachian Highlands Association, national advisor, 1975–1980

Southern Appalachian Highlands Conservancy, founding board member, vice president, 1974–1978

North Carolina Land Heritage Trust (later merged into North Carolina Nature Conservancy), founder, 1975–1980

NC Nature Conservancy, co-founder, 1977

American Farmland Trust, National Advisory Committee, 1983–1996

China Poot Bay Society, Alaska, member, 1988–1997

National Committee for the New River, Land Trust Committee, Board of Governors, 1994–1999

Woods Hole Oceanographic Institution, WHOI Corp., Development Committee, 1994–1997

Agri-Systems Research and Extension Network of North America, member Founding Committee, 1995

Blue Ridge Parkway, Council of Advisors, 1999–

New River (Va.) Blueway, initiator, 2002

Blue Ridge Rural Land Trust, Advisory Board, 2003–

The H.J. Heinz Center for Science, Economics, and the Environment, Development Committee, 2004–

AWARDS

The North Carolina and National Wildlife Federation Award for Preservation of Natural Areas, 1969

The Gulf Oil and Isaac Walton League of America Conservation Award, 1982

Honorary North Carolina Park Ranger, Naturalist, 1990

Honorary Commander, *USS North Carolina*, 1998

OTHER

North Carolina Society of New York, Resident Advisory Board,
1985

Old Salem, Inc., Development Committee, board member,
1974–1977

Salem College and Academy, trustee, 1961–1964

Salem College, vice chairman Arts Center Fund Drive, 1965

Winston-Salem Total Development Committee, vice chairman,
1960–1962

Sparta Memorial Hospital, trustee, 1965

Chatham Memorial Hospital, trustee, 1965

Forsyth Economic Development Corp., director, 1969–1971

J. W. and A. H. Hanes Foundation, director, 1974–

Southeastern Council on Foundations, member, 1975–1980

Young Presidents Organization, 1956–1975

Chief Executives Forum, member, 1975–1977

World Business Council, member, 1976–1978

Enterprise Foundation, Advisory Board, 1981

Ordine dei Cavalieri del Raviolo e del Cortese, 1994

Virginia Polytechnic Institute, Ut Prosim Society, member, 1993

Year of the Mountains Commission, appointed by Governor
Hunt, 1995

Special Olympics World Games, Chairman's Cabinet, 1998–1999

Piedmont Triad Partnership, board, 2004-

CLUBS

Bohemian Club (California); Metropolitan (Washington); Century, Lotos, Yale (New York); Confrérie de la Chaîne des Rôtisseurs; Cane River Fishing, Currituck Shooting (North Carolina); Peale (Philadelphia); Piedmont Club; Twin City Club

BIOGRAPHY

HANES, Ralph Philip, Jr., textile company executive; b. Winston-Salem, N.C., February 25, 1926; s. Ralph Philip and DeWitt (Chatham); h. graduated Woodberry Forest School, 1944; student, UNC, 1944–1946; graduated Yale University (Whiffenpoof) (DKE) (BA degree), 1947–1949; m. Joan Audrey Humpstone, January 14, 1950 (d) 1983; m. Mary Charlotte Metz, December 23, 1984; Lt. USNR-R; Hanes Companies, Inc., Winston-Salem, N.C., 1950–1993; Chairman of the Board, 1978–1988; Chairman Emeritus, 1989–

Listed in: *Who's Who in America, Who's Who in the World, Who's Who in 20th Century America, International Directory of Distinguished Leadership*

■ ■ ■

Immortality is assured
by how many lives you've touched.

—ANON

AFTERWORD

Age may wrinkle your brow but it should never wrinkle your heart. The spirit should never grow old.

—PRESIDENT JAMES A. GARFIELD

Frank Jones, a marvelous photographer for the *Winston-Salem Journal*, was an outrageous character whose epitaph reads, "He lived until he died." Could any of us ask for better?

Some people, as they grow older, just keep doing what they've always done. A prime example is Ted Stern, who took the College of Charleston from about 500 students to 4,500. He was also the founding chairman of Charleston's Spoleto Festival, managing both the festival and the mercurial Gian Carlo Menotti for nearly fifteen years. In his late seventies, Ted moved to a small farm on the Blue Ridge Parkway just a hoot and a holler from Sparta "to take life easier," which included revitalizing the local chamber of commerce and creating the Bank of Sparta. At eighty-eight, he raised $7 million for a new library at the College of Charleston. After celebrating his ninetieth birthday, he told me he was finally slowing down. "Now I can do only eighty push-ups from the toes," he confided.

It seems to me that a person who has finished his or her chores during their first sixty-five years is now prepared to stop "doing" and start "accomplishing"—that is, you can accomplish by persuading others to do the doing and use your accumulated knowledge and experience to back up the doers.

I waited until I was seventy-five to begin putting all of my resources to work, vowing that the next ten years would be my most productive. With the assistance of my two powerful allies—my wife Charlotte and my partner Chris Griffith—I have seen a rebirth of downtown Winston-Salem. New restaurants, cafes, bars, clubs, shops, galleries, and performance spaces vie for attention along tree-lined sidewalks. The city's inspectors are friends and allies to local entrepreneurs instead of adversaries. We've formed a Restaurant and Club Roundtable where owners and managers meet monthly to share mutual concerns, pool resources for advertising and promotion, and listen to experts from other regions of the state and country. Thanks to our Downtown Winston-Salem Partnership, low-interest loans are available to all kinds of businesses and enterprises that would ordinarily have a hard time getting started. Through our network, experts and fellow business owners offer free advice, support, and even financial coaching to help new establishments get off the ground.

In addition, Charlotte and I are saving as much land as we can along the New River that flows south to north from North Carolina to West Virginia. To date, we've purchased 1,200 acres with 250 cow/calf pairs, plus bulls. Thanks to the sage advice of Vaughn Jones, we both practice and teach the New Zealand method of low-input intensive rotational grazing with our cattle, which uses very little hay, machinery, fertilizer, or antibiotics and absolutely no grain feed or hormones. Twenty other farmers have joined our program, some from as far away as Richmond, a hundred miles distant.

We are currently building a land conservation organization to acquire easements and have just raised $50,000 from the Fish and Wildlife Foundation to hire a manager. We played a major part in having the New River declared an American Heritage River and persuaded President Clinton and Vice President Gore to make the dedication in a pasture on the river bank. (When I extended the invitation, I learned that the president never made personal appearances without a guarantee of at least 10,000 people in attendance; our audience of 13,000 stomped that pasture flat.)

Never doubt that a small group of committed people can change the world. Indeed, it is the only thing that ever has.

—MARGARET MEAD

These and numerous other projects occupy me seven days a week. Now in my eightieth year, I am not only at my most productive, but also I'm having a ball. I think of Fred Crawford, at age one hundred, and still active on the Woods Hole Oceanographic Institute; of Lawrence Ferlinghetti, at eighty-five, and still running his renowned City Lights Bookstore in San Francisco while continuing to paint and give poetry readings around the world; of architect Lawrence Halprin, the designer of San Francisco's famed Ghirardelli Square, vest-pocket parks in New York, and the Roosevelt Memorial, and finally completing a new entrance for Yosemite National Park at the age of eighty-five; of his wife Anna, founding director of the Anna Halprin Dance Company, who performed her most famous piece of choreography on the London stage at the age of eighty-two; and of President Reagan, who didn't do so badly in his seventies, proudly boasting that he could still put on his socks without having to sit down.

David Rockefeller, now in his nineties, completed his autobiography in his late eighties, and had this to say about commitment: "Philanthropy is involved with basic innovations that transform society, not simply maintaining the status quo nor simply filling basic needs that were formerly the province of the public sector."

■ THE ONLY WAY TO GET THE MOST OUT OF LIFE ■
IS TO GIVE THE MOST.

When you stop giving, when you stop working for the general weal, you become boring and dull and—yes—old. Youth is not a period of life that comes to an inevitable end; it is a state of mind—strengthened by will, inspired by emotion. It is the triumph of daring over timidity, of thirst for adventure over convenience. Old age is not a matter of years, but only a matter of loss and/or renunciation of ideals.

I believe that being young means to retain, at the age of sixty or seventy or eighty or more, a love of wonder, a rapture in the presence of new ideals, a longing for fresh challenges, and a feeling of pleasure and joy in the shining presence of timeless truths.

To stay young, we must learn to grasp those messages of beauty, audacity, and courage that come from the Infinite and reveal their greatness and strength. When your heart is broken, your shoulders sink and your enthusiasm cools under the snows of cynicism; only then can you consider yourself old and may the Almighty have mercy on your soul.

In times such as these, it is no failure to fall short of all that we might dream—the failure is to fall short of dreaming all that we might realize.

—DEE HOCK, Birth of the Chaordic Age

One of my editors, Frances Bowles, asked me "What do you think of the notion that networking is just a euphemism for using people?" (She really likes that word. I, too, love a euphemism, as long as I don't get any of it on me.) She made a good point and my answer was, "I absolutely agree! And when networking uses people, it can be evil and Machiavellian. But not the way I do it."

At my daily prayers I ask for a blessing on my dreams or, conversely, an abrupt end to an unworthy project. My aim is to empower and encourage others to accomplish projects that are suited to their talents but which, initially, may seem too large to be successfully undertaken. In the end, I want them to get the credit. That's the way it should be because that's the way to spread the work around within a community.

For example, I know I was responsible for assembling the land (including my gift of 1,100 acres) for Stone Mountain Park, North Carolina's largest state park. But the road into the park was named for the CEO of the mining company that owned the mountain and sold it to the state (at a considerable profit). My name is so far unmentioned. I raised the $3 million that made possible Winston-Salem's largest hotel, the Adam's Mark. The chamber of commerce celebrated the hotel's completion by presenting a community award to our mayor, who oversaw the project. My name is still unconnected.

But the recognition comes eventually in different and unexpected ways; the generous and anonymous donor is never really anonymous for long. (Mr. Woodruff of Coca Cola in Atlanta always made his donations anonymously, but he was so generous—he became known as "Mr. Anonymous.")

To me what matters is seeing the successful fulfillment of a dream. In a way, this book is a memoir of a fantastic life that has been filled with dreams, mine as well as others. Along the way, new territory was explored and opportunities grasped. And perhaps the most fortuitous events were the failures. When I learned that failure is not the end of the rope, only a knot along its length—a knot that may be used as a hand-hold before reaching higher—I learned I could take chances, leave the well-trodden trail and pursue distant goals.

My uncle, Dr. Fred Hanes, who founded the Duke Medical School, said, "To prepare your children for life, plan a failure or disappointment every day."

A SHAGGY DOG TALE

Process is more important than outcome. When the outcome drives the process, we will only ever go to where we've already been.

If process drives outcome, we may not know where we're going; but we'll know we want to be there.

—Bruce Mau, "An Incomplete Manifesto for Growth"

When I told some friends that I was writing this book, they all said, "Great idea!" I passed this response along to Phil Wood, owner and publisher of Ten Speed Press, who encouraged me to proceed.

I was introduced to Penelope (Penny) Niven, whose biographies of Carl Sandburg, James Earl Jones, Edward Steichen and, soon to come, Thornton Wilder, have met with great success. She agreed to lunch with me and help me find an editor. After lunch she said, "I want to edit that book." (Penny says that she is walking testimony to the success of my strategies: before she knew it, I had persuaded her she should be my editor.) Together we approached an important New York City agent, Barbara Hogenson, who, upon learning about the book's content, said, "I want to read it myself."

As I complete this, my first book, I am reminded of the original shaggy dog story, to wit: A man had bought a dog and was taking him for a walk when several people came up to him and said, "That is a truly shaggy dog! You should enter him in the shaggy dog contest." Upon making inquires, he learned that there was indeed a National Shaggy Dog Contest, and so he and the dog flew to New York and went to the contest headquarters. Upon entering the reception room, the man was asked the purpose of his visit. He pointed to his dog. The receptionist said, "So?"

The man responded that he wanted to enter the dog in the Shaggy Dog Contest. The receptionist took a second look and responded emphatically, "That dog ain't shaggy!"

After reading these anecdotes, I hope you find herein some fresh approaches to making contacts, taking risks, raising money, solving problems, and working with those who work with and for you. Those who have encouraged me are the true judges of the quality of these ideas. And I hope that you do, indeed, find this dog to be shaggy.

INDEX